ADVANCE PRAISE FOR
TIRED OF TRYING

Our greatest disappointments, deepest pain, and disillusionments—
things that shake us and break us and make us wonder about
everything—don't have to mean all hope is lost. When we're tired
of trying and tired of hoping, I love that my friend Ashley helps
us see that we might be in the middle of the wrestling. And I want
to wrestle well and come out renewed, even when it's painful. This
book will help you with that and more. Get your copy and settle in
because it's that good!

LYSA TERKEURST,
#1 *New York Times* bestselling author;
president of Proverbs 31 Ministries

If you, too, are disappointed and exhausted, feel like you are in a
season of wrestling with God, and are just tired of trying, this book
may be the prescription you need to release, rest, and revive your
passion for life. Ashley vulnerably shares her personal journey of
pain, discovery, and healing in easy-to-read pages that are saturated
in God's Word and dripping with hope.

GINGER STACHE,
author of *Chasing Wonder: Small Steps
toward a Life of Big Adventures*

This is a *must-read* when life feels tiring and purpose seems elusive.
This is the reminder we all need (and are desperately looking for)
in the middle of the fight to keep going, wrestling, and waiting on
God to do what only He can do. Like a friend, Ashley encourages

us at every turn: Showing up to the fight is not only worth it, but blessing is coming—and *I am here for it.*

HEIDI LEE ANDERSON,
author of *P.S. It's Gonna Be Good: How God's Word Answers Our Questions about Faith, Fear, and All the Things*; popular Christian content creator @heidileeanderson and @thismotherhen

Ashley Morgan Jackson allows us to peer into those moments most of us want to hide—the times when we are tired of trying and at the end of our rope. She shares her experiences so we don't feel alone in our trying loops, and she gives us practical tools to help realign our skewed perspectives. If you are tired of trying, get this book today!

MELISSA SPOELSTRA,
Bible study teacher and author of *Isaiah: Striving Less and Trusting God More*

If you are tired of trying to do things by digging in your heels and sounding like a toddler in the Target toy aisle, then you will want to read this book! I was around during Ashley's dark wrestling years when God was growing her more each day. She shares in her book how she looks back on that time with empathy and grace for herself while also seeing how that really hard time grew her inner spirit. You will want to root for her while you also identify with her raw experiences and emotions. Ashley has never had it all together (just like the rest of us), but her example will inspire you to never stop trying.

DR. LINDSAY DEIBLER,
clinical psychologist; drlindsaydeibler.com

As one who grew up in a Christian tradition where admitting any frustration or anger with God was a big no-no, I love that Ashley Morgan Jackson puts the realities of the Christian life on full display. While brilliantly weaving in Jacob's story of wrestling with God, Ashley gives voice to the dark questions, deep fears, and life-giving truth about a God who sees and cares. Ashley will lead you to confront the hard things that are holding you back by pointing you to God's truth and teaching you to trust His loving heart.

BARB ROOSE,
speaker; author of *Surrendered: Letting Go and Living Like Jesus*

I didn't know how much I needed this book until I began reading it and tears filled my eyes while going through almost every chapter. As Ashley vulnerably shares about her own process of wrestling with the Lord, she creates a safe place for you to do the same—to feel, process, wrestle, and truly have honest conversations with Him. This idea of wrestling with the Lord is biblical, and I believe it's not talked about enough in the church. God can handle your questions and your disappointments—and when you bring all of that to Him, He's not angry or impatient; He's loving, steadfast, and truly working on your behalf to turn what the enemy meant for evil into good.

LAUREN SMITH,
worship leader and songwriter, New Life Church, Colorado Springs, CO

Tired of Trying is an answered prayer for those of us in the middle of a wrestling season. I love how, instead of running away from it, Ashley authentically shares her own story and how she breaks down the story of Jacob wrestling with God. In doing so, she invites us to shift our perspective on struggling—that God isn't doing this to us; instead He's using it to transform us. I know you'll love this book as much as I did!

LEANNA CRAWFORD,
artist/songwriter

Such an incredibly personal, heartfelt, and challenging book. Ashley unpacks the story of Jacob's wrestle in such a beautiful way that invites us into a life of embracing the wrestle rather than trying to get away from it. *Tired of Trying* is filled with practical thoughts and truths that help us change our perspective and walk into the joy and blessing that God has for us. It's easy to find yourself in her struggle but also feel the weight of "trying" begin to lift as she shares her story to find wholeness and freedom.

DONNA LASIT,
lead pastor, The Pearl Church,
Denver, CO

Ashley Morgan Jackson is one of the most incredibly brave, courageous, and compassionate souls I know. In her book, *Tired of Trying*, she not only made me feel like I had a friend sitting right beside me, but she was also that friend we all need—the one who says, "Come on, I love you enough to not let you stay in this place." She writes with deep authenticity and grace. This is a must-have resource for every woman who is desperately trying to follow after Jesus but feels like it's one big wrestling match.

NICKI KOZIARZ,
bestselling author and speaker,
Proverbs 31 Ministries

This is the book you read when you are struggling with feeling let down by God. This is for the woman who is being attacked by her own thoughts. Ashley Morgan Jackson speaks to your pain with the compassion of a friend who has been there. She knows the way out—even when you are tired of trying.

HEATHER THOMPSON DAY,
author of *It's Not Your Turn: What to Do While You're Waiting for Your Breakthrough*

TIRED OF TRYING

TIRED OF TRYING
TIRED OF TRYIN
TIRED OF TRYI
TIRED OF TRY
TIRED OF TR
TIRED OF T
TIRED OF
TIRED O
TIRED

HOW TO HOLD ON TO GOD WHEN YOU'RE FRUSTRATED, FED UP & FEELING FORGOTTEN

ASHLEY MORGAN JACKSON

TYNDALE
MOMENTUM®

A Tyndale nonfiction imprint

Visit Tyndale online at tyndale.com.

Visit Tyndale Momentum online at tyndalemomentum.com.

Tyndale, Tyndale's quill logo, *Tyndale Momentum*, and the Tyndale Momentum logo are registered trademarks of Tyndale House Ministries. Tyndale Momentum is a nonfiction imprint of Tyndale House Publishers, Carol Stream, Illinois.

This book is dedicated to Jesus, the one my soul loves, who has been with me from my first breath, who has stayed with me through every struggle, and who refused to let me go until He blessed me. You are worth it all. We did it, Lord. I love you so much.

CONTENTS

TIRED OF TRYING
TIRED OF TRYIN
TIRED OF TRYI
TIRED OF TRY
TIRED OF TR
TIRED OF T
TIRED OF
TIRED O
TIRED

AN INVITATION TO THE WRESTLE

Once you've wrestled, everything else in life is easy.
DAN GABLE,
Olympic gold medal wrestler and coach

ROLLING OVER ONTO MY SIDE, I picked up my phone from the nightstand. I checked my social media first thing every morning like it was an uncontrollable impulse, but now even the thought of doing so felt like it was raising my blood pressure. I knew what waited for me there—other people enjoying their lives while I cried about mine. I put the phone back on the nightstand and dragged my exhausted body out of bed to attend to my baby son, whom I was sure I was unfit to parent.

As I crossed the room and passed the full-length mirror, I caught a glimpse of myself sporting three-day unwashed hair and the mismatched pajamas I had dug out of the bottom dresser drawer the night before. I wished I hadn't seen that discouraging sight—more proof of the disappointment I believed I was. I paused, slowly inhaling and then exhaling with a long sigh. Sighing was one of the only things that lightened the pressure I always felt in my chest. But the relief lasted only for a moment, so I found myself sighing often. Hot tears filled my eyes, and I immediately tried to blink them back.

I couldn't be starting that so early today. *Press on, Ashley. Push through, even if no one knows or cares.* In fact, I was convinced that no one did care and that everyone I knew was sick of me. I understood how they felt because I was sick of me too.

I walked down the hall to my son's room, picked him up, and carried him to the living room. After setting him on a blanket on the floor, I plopped down on the couch behind him and rubbed my temples while staring at the carpet. *Am I going to feel like this forever?* My heart was racing wildly, as if I had just finished a brisk jog, but I couldn't remember the last time I had run. Who had the time to care about exercise? Forget the time; just, who cared—period?

Not me.

I told myself I didn't care about anything, but the truth was, I did care—a lot. Maybe not about running, but I cared deeply, obsessively, about other things. I cared what everyone thought of me, even strangers. I cared about whether I mattered, why I felt so rejected, and why my mind felt like it was broken. Most of all, I cared about why God seemed to have left me to deal with all of this alone.

My mind felt like an enemy. *How do I get away from an enemy I carry around with me at all times?* I was battling depression and anxiety, both of which were squeezing the life out of me. There were days I sobbed on the kitchen floor as my husband crouched next to me, beside himself with worry and concern. I had panic attacks that happened at the most inconvenient and inappropriate times, including one time when we went to the mall. I had to run out because I couldn't handle all the people and the pressure to keep it together. As we quickly made our way out of the parking lot, I had to roll down the car window to get some air because I couldn't breathe. Tears streamed down my face and humiliation rushed through my body. I felt like everyone knew I was as broken and weird as I had become.

I felt ashamed of myself because I thought I was an embarrassment to my family.

As time went by, I began to realize that this wasn't just a passing case of baby blues. The hard days that had turned into hard weeks and then hard months had changed me into someone I no longer recognized. This was not who I had been. The girl I had been was adventurous and confident. She loved the Lord with all her heart and was ready to go to the ends of the earth for Him. I had spent years becoming that girl, and that was who I still wanted to be. That was the identity in which I found my validation, the identity in which I felt safe and secure. I didn't know who this new girl was, but I hated her. My carefully crafted image had crumbled to pieces.

If I'm being honest, I felt let down by God, like He hadn't held up His end of the bargain. I wanted Him to get me back to the girl I once was. I wanted Him to help me become the strong version of myself that was respected and much easier to love. Why wasn't He doing what I so desperately wanted Him to do? I wrestled between feeling like God had hurt my feelings and knowing that wasn't possible. An ache shot through me as I wondered how I could feel so betrayed by a God I loved so much.

All the prayers I had prayed, all the Bible verses I had memorized, all the "good things" I knew to do now exhausted me. I felt like a hamster on a wheel—I was running hard but getting nowhere and starting to resent it. I was frustrated and tired of trying.

For five years, God brought me through what I can only describe as a wrestling season. I didn't want to be there, I never signed up for it, and I resented every moment of it. And yet, there I was. And I had a choice to make—I could either hold on to God when I was full of fear, frustrated with how it was all going, and fed up with things that wouldn't change, or I could let the growing resentment I felt toward

Him put down bitter roots in my heart. I also had questions to face. Could God handle what was really in my heart? Could I be honest with Him about the pain and frustration I felt? Did my inability to get myself together or have enough faith make me offensive to Him? Would He reject me?

I said I trusted God, but the truth was I trusted Him to do things my way, in my time. That changed during my wrestling season when God asked me to trust Him moment by moment and choice by choice, with no guarantees about what the outcome might be. He asked me to bring all my pains, all my fears, and all my doubts so we could grapple with them together. He asked me to voice my belief that He was letting me down, and to struggle through it with Him. I did not have to pretend I was strong or perform for His love and acceptance. I didn't have to hide that I thought my circumstances were unfair and that I was struggling. The choice was inevitable: Would I dare to run *to* Him with my wounds and questions or would I run *from* Him and let my heart grow calloused?

> I said I trusted God, but the truth was I trusted Him to do things my way, in my time.

YOU'RE INVITED

Maybe you've had feelings like these too. You might even admit that you're a little mad at God right now. If so, you are not alone. I know your pain all too well—the pain of wondering why God is letting it hurt. I know how lonely that place can be.

In case you need the reminder, it is absolutely okay that you feel "over it" and like your pain has stolen the best of who you are. I'm sorry you've been hurting so deeply and for so long. I know you expected to handle this better, to be stronger when everything came crashing down; but it's okay that you're feeling weak and unsure. You're not superwoman; you're just a girl who is hurting deeply and who needs her Savior. You are not an inconvenience to God, and He is not annoyed when you feel fearful, fed up, and forgotten.

When we reach the place where the only choice is to run to God or run from Him, God invites us to hold on to Him even tighter—to wrestle with Him. It's an invitation God first gave to the biblical character Jacob. When Jacob was in the most painful and difficult season of his life, he pleaded with God for rescue. Instead of rushing in to save him, God's answer to Jacob's prayer was to invite him to a wrestle.

> **Y**ou are not an inconvenience to God, and He is not annoyed when you feel fearful, fed up, and forgotten.

We may be invited to wrestle when we are grappling with a loss, a struggle, or feeling stuck. Wrestling might be the choice we have to make when we face the death of a dream, buckle under the weight of a long-carried grief, or feel overlooked and left behind. Or we may have to hold on to God in the face of something we never saw coming—a crisis that became a constant burden and is now our daily life, an unexpected broken heart, or a wait that never seems to end.

The kind of wrestle that God invites us to is not easy or quick. It requires us to continue to bring our hearts to God as we navigate the painful chasm between how life was supposed to be and how it is. But this wrestling has a purpose. God never requires anything from us that is not for our good, for the outworking of His Kingdom, and for the glory of His name.

We may know the following promise well, but it's especially important to remember it when we're wrestling: "And we know that for those who love God all things work together for good, for those who are called according to his purpose" (Romans 8:28). When we enter a wrestling season, we just have to keep holding on to see Him do that work.

What does it look like to keep holding on? Jacob's story shows us. Although he was tired of trying, Jacob was also determined to receive a blessing from the one who met him in his struggle. Scripture describes Jacob's wrestle in just six verses:

> So Jacob was left alone, and a man wrestled with him till daybreak. When the man saw that he could not overpower him, he touched the socket of Jacob's hip so that his hip was wrenched as he wrestled with the man. Then the man said, "Let me go, for it is daybreak."
>
> But Jacob replied, "I will not let you go unless you bless me."
>
> The man asked him, "What is your name?"
>
> "Jacob," he answered.
>
> Then the man said, "Your name will no longer be Jacob, but Israel, because you have struggled with God and with humans and have overcome."
>
> Jacob said, "Please tell me your name."
>
> But he replied, "Why do you ask my name?" Then he blessed him there.
>
> GENESIS 32:24-29, NIV

After a long, dark night of struggling with God and holding on to Him, Jacob emerged with a limp but also with a new identity, a new future, and God's promised blessing. Jacob's struggle with God had a purpose; it was a transformation process God designed for Jacob's good.

There are many lessons we can learn from Jacob as we enter into our own seasons of wrestling, including how to let go of who we thought we were and how life was supposed to go according to our plan. As Jacob did, we, too, can make the hard choices to engage God, to learn through our struggles with God, and to experience the freedom and blessing that come from surrendering to God's way.

So what about you? No matter how unstable your faith may feel, no matter how tired you might be from trying things that have left you feeling empty, know today that your story is far from over. God doesn't invite you to wrestle because you are bad or because He is mean, but because He wants to show you things and give you things that will bless you—things you can't see or receive any other way. And that is what I pray this book will reveal to you.

Like Jacob, when we are in our deepest pain, we can choose to hang on to our good and capable God as we boldly cry out for help. As we wrestle, we learn how to let go of our need to perform for God and discover how to let Him love us just as we are—fears, frustrations, and all. The Lord can do more with our honest pleas for help than our forced performances. Sometimes the best prayers we can pray are the simple ones: "This hurts. I'm scared. Please help."

This is your invitation to the wrestle—the choice to face God in your greatest fears, pains, and unanswered questions.

HOW TO READ *TIRED OF TRYING*

Tired of Trying includes practical and spiritual guidance to help you wrestle well. The chapters explore the hard choices we must make, the struggles we must face, and the blessings we can expect when we accept God's invitation to the wrestle. Throughout, I will be sharing my own wrestle and we will also gain insights from the story of Jacob, the first human being to wrestle with God and come through blessed like never before.

To help you get the most out of each chapter, I've included

reflection questions at the back of the book. Because the wrestle is a journey of self-discovery, you may also find it helpful to jot down notes in a journal as you read or to write your thoughts in the margins. If you begin to recall previous hardships and seasons of wrestling with God, use your journal to reflect on how God was faithful to you in the past and how you grew or changed as a result. This may be a source of encouragement to you as you wrestle with God again now. I also encourage you to consider inviting a trusted friend or small group to read with you. Wrestling together is easier than wrestling alone.

Similar to an actual wrestling match that has three rounds, *Tired of Trying* is laid out in three parts. In Part 1: Hard Choices, we start where we are and not where we wish we were. That requires clarifying what is exhausting you spiritually when you are tired from all your trying. We will learn why making hard choices is essential to wrestling well.

In Part 2: Struggling with God, we consider both the good and the hard of holding on to God with all we have. You'll discover why God invites you to wrestle, the good He is working on your behalf as you hold on, the old identities you need to let go of, and the beautiful importance of holding on to Him until you receive a blessing.

In Part 3: The Blessings of Being Broken, we explore how the choice to wrestle forever changes us and how we can learn to trust Him in new and bold ways. The most beautiful thing of all happens on the other side of the wrestle—we receive a blessing we could never have experienced without it. God invites us to wrestle so He can do in us what cannot be done in any other way. Then we have the opportunity to leave a legacy by passing that blessing on to others.

My hope and prayer is that you will accept this invitation to wrestle even though you are so tired of trying. I believe you've got some fight left in you, and this is how I know—because you picked up this book. You are not done, and God is not done with you. Jesus died so you could have every spiritual blessing He has for you; don't settle for less.

The psalmist wrote, "Even though I walk through the darkest valley, I will fear no evil, for you are with me" (Psalm 23:4, NIV). That's a promise you can claim as your own.

Let's walk through your darkest valley together and let God do what He has come to do.

PART 1

HARD CHOICES

WHEN YOU'RE FRUSTRATED

Anger and frustration are the result of you not
being authentic somewhere in your life or with
someone in your life. Being fake about anything
creates a block inside of you. Life can't work
for you if you don't show up as you.

JASON MRAZ,
guitarist, singer, and songwriter

I WAS SITTING IN THE FRONT PASSENGER SEAT, and my husband was driving. Drowning in anxiety, I dug my nails into my forearm as firmly as I could, scratching myself repeatedly. I wanted to feel anything other than what I was feeling inside. When the scratching didn't bring relief, I began punching myself in the leg as hard as I could. My husband noticed and grabbed my hand to stop me. Sitting behind us in the backseat were my two-year-old son and my parents. I both did and didn't want them to see what I was doing.

My frustration demanded to be expressed. I was furious with myself for being so broken, so weak, so unfaithful to God, so impossible to love. I was desperate to be loved in spite of it all, but I wondered if it was even possible to be loved when I had nothing to offer. The torment of not knowing had led to this moment, which had been a long time coming. This was not the way my life was supposed to be, and this was not how I was supposed to feel. I had tried everything I could think of to fix myself—prayer, listening to sermons, memorizing Bible verses, and serving more at church. I was convinced I was only worth hating, and my response to that pain was crying all the time. Inside, I was screaming at the top of my lungs, but no one could hear me. It was like being encased in a glass box; people could see me, but they just looked at me blankly, not understanding what I was trying to communicate.

My mental chatter was nonstop. *Don't be so needy. No one likes a needy person, Ashley. Just fix yourself, just be strong, just read more books, or better yet, read more of the Bible. Just do it! Hurry up! Your brokenness is such an inconvenience.*

I had been trying hard not to be depressed, trying hard not to have anxiety attacks, and trying hardest of all to escape this torment that was in my mind. I had been trying hard for the past two years, and I was desperate for relief, for answers, and for rescue. I was being chased by all the emotions rushing through me, and I needed somewhere to hide from it all. My mind screamed, *Do something! Anything! Stop being such a stupid, difficult human being. You are useless, you are alone, and you deserve pain!* I wasn't sure how much longer I could tolerate the internal screams, each one cutting like a knife. I didn't want the screams to be true, but I was terrified they were.

I was desperate to be saved, and I wanted my family to save me. They did try to help in their own way, but they were at a loss for what to do. I couldn't find any logic or reason for what I was going through. *If only I could fix myself and be the perfect daughter, sister, aunt, friend, mother, wife, and Christian everyone needs me to be, maybe things will get "back to normal."* But that was the problem. There were no more fixes, and I simply could not try anymore. I had nothing left. And if I couldn't be perfect, why try at all?

My husband parked the car in front of my brother's new house.

The surrounding neighborhood was picturesque on that October afternoon, with fall leaves lining the street and perfectly manicured yards in front of every home. All the tidy order felt like such a stark contrast to the mess that was flailing inside of me, and something in me snapped. I threw open the car door and started running down the street.

My family didn't get it, and I had to get away. I had no idea where I was running, and I could hear angry voices behind me calling me to come back. I knew annoyance and disappointment were waiting for me back there, and I couldn't face it. *How can I explain to them something I can't even put words around myself?*

I hadn't gone very far before I was out of breath. Everyone knows you can't cry and run—well, maybe only those of us who have ever dared to try. Slowing down to catch my breath and wipe away the tears streaming down my face, I noticed a neighborhood park and ended up sitting in a small gazebo. My dad walked down the street after me, upset and angry. He didn't understand this strange behavior any more than I did, and I felt helpless to explain it to him. All I wanted was for him to look me in the eyes and tell me everything was going to be alright, to see past my anger and strange actions, to acknowledge my pain, and to tell me he loved me.

I couldn't help but long for the simplicity of childhood, a time when things seemed to make more sense. When I was in pain, my parents were there to help me feel better, not to tell me to get over it. Now, I believed all I had ever known was lost, and I had to somehow find my way back to reality on my own. *Isn't my family supposed to help make it all better? Why won't they save me?*

I was trapped in frustration. I was frustrated that my parents couldn't help me and even more frustrated that I couldn't help myself. I wanted to be the one who could snap her fingers, read the right verses, or pray the right prayers, and all of this would be better.

Nothing I tried, nothing I prayed, nothing I conveyed to other people, none of the ways I tried to avoid or escape my problems worked. *Why wasn't anything working?* All the strategies that I'd used in the past led only to dead ends. *Was it something I was doing, not doing, had done? Was this from sin? Was this a punishment? Was God mad at me?* If only I could figure out how to learn the lesson I was supposed to learn from this season, then maybe I could be free of it.

Instead, I felt trapped under the weight of frustration and pain that was largely invisible to everyone around me—and pain that is not acknowledged or understood is pain that crushes the soul. Because my pain was unseen and others could not understand it, I let myself believe my emotional reactions were illogical, inappropriate, and uncalled for.

Pain that is not acknowledged or understood is pain that crushes the soul.

Your circumstances are no doubt different from mine, but I'm guessing one aspect of it may feel familiar—the frustration. Maybe you are frustrated that you feel desperate, helpless, hopeless, scared, or enraged. Perhaps you have even reached the point of being just plain done. You're looking for a way out or a way through. Whatever it is, you're sure it needs to happen now.

So why does God allow painful and disorienting seasons like these in our lives? What is their purpose, and how can we recognize when we are entering into one? No matter how desperate we are to escape the frustration, the most important thing we can do at this point is to get to know it better. Why? Because when we can define the frustration, we can better recognize the wrestle. Sometimes, our frustration is what points us to the issue God is asking us to look at and address.

LEARNING FROM JACOB'S FRUSTRATION

Jacob was no stranger to frustration. In fact, it had been building up throughout the nine decades of his life that led up to his wrestle with God. To understand how this happened, we need to look back to his beginnings.

Things were complicated for Jacob from the start. And by start, I mean in the womb. When Rebekah was pregnant with Jacob and his twin, Esau, Scripture says,

> The children struggled together within her, and she said, "If it is thus, why is this happening to me?" So she went to inquire of the Lord. And the Lord said to her,

> "Two nations are in your womb,
>   and two peoples from within you shall be divided;
> the one shall be stronger than the other,
>   the older shall serve the younger."

GENESIS 25:22-23

These words are important to remember because Rebekah held them close to her heart. She knew God was proclaiming that Jacob, her younger son, would lead. In the years to come, she would take drastic and misguided measures to make sure this promise was fulfilled.

Shortly after Rebekah received the Lord's words, the twins were delivered. Esau was born first but Jacob came out grasping his brother's heel. As a result, he was given the name Jacob, meaning, "one who follows on another's heels; supplanter."[1] We don't really use the word *supplanter* much today, so if you're wondering what that means, here's how the dictionary defines it: "someone or something taking the place of another, as through force, scheming, strategy, or the like."[2] In other words, from the moment he was born, Jacob was a schemer and a cheat.

Can you imagine being defined this way from the moment you

7

were born? Perhaps when you've always been defined by a weakness and the shame associated with it, the only real option is to live up to that identity—which Jacob did. Here is perhaps the first indicator we have about the source of Jacob's frustration: "When the boys grew up, Esau was a skillful hunter, a man of the field, while Jacob was a quiet man, dwelling in tents. Isaac loved Esau because he ate of his game, but Rebekah loved Jacob" (Genesis 25:27-28). Did Jacob have resentment toward his father for this lack of love and therefore feel frustrated at being second best to his brother?

With this first frustration in mind, we run right into a second—wondering when God's promise to his mother would be fulfilled. I can imagine Jacob and Rebekah preparing meals together day after day, wondering when and how God would follow through. As the years passed, Jacob and his mother likely felt a growing frustration about when this would take place. When they got tired of waiting, they reasoned that the only way forward was to take matters into their own hands to secure God's promised blessing for Jacob.

The first part of Jacob's plan was to trick his brother, Esau, out of his birthright. One day, when Esau came home exhausted and famished from being in the open country, he begged for a bowl of the stew Jacob was cooking. "First sell me your birthright," Jacob responded (Genesis 25:31, NIV). The birthright was the double portion of the family inheritance, and Esau swore an oath to sell his birthright for the stew. But Jacob also needed the blessing of his father in order to receive what God had promised. That's when he and his mother hatched a scheme to get it. Jacob tricked Isaac, his elderly and blind father, into giving him the blessing by pretending to be Esau (Genesis 27:28-29).

Jacob's actions reveal that he was frustrated with God. He feared God had forgotten His promise, and His apparent inaction only increased Jacob's mounting frustration. So Jacob relied on his scheming skills to make things happen and get the blessing for himself. Undefined and unaddressed frustration almost always leads us to take misguided actions in order to find relief.

FACING FRUSTRATION

Each of us deals differently with our frustration with God. Perhaps "checking out" is your go-to strategy. If there is no solution and you don't seem to be getting any help, then your frustration unfolds as indifference. You reason that the solution is to ignore God since He appears to be ignoring you.

Or maybe your heart is shattered, and your frustration shows up as anger. God's silence and inaction have hurt your feelings. It no longer feels safe to express your pain, so you are quick to lash out at those around you. If you're honest, you believe God just doesn't love you enough to care whether you react one way or another.

Perhaps you've learned to cope by getting busy and trying even harder. Feeling overwhelmed, stressed out, or anxious is your cue to pray harder, serve harder, read the Bible more faithfully. Surely God will see how hard you're trying and come through at last, right?

Or maybe when you start to feel sad, depressed, or forgotten by God, your default is to find some way to "numb out." It might be overindulging in junk food, shopping for things you don't need, binge-watching reality television, playing with electronic gadgets, or misusing your substance of choice.

In my five years of feeling let down by God, I cycled through each of these frustration management strategies. My inability to find relief turned to deep depression, my thoughts constantly churning over what an awful person I was for not being the capable individual I had always considered myself to be. But no matter how hard I looked for solutions, I couldn't fix myself and I had no idea why.

My frustration led me to question God.

Why are you being so mean?

Are you doing this on purpose?

Where are you? I need you!

I'm guessing you have your own frustrating thoughts and questions as hot tears roll down your cheeks on yet another night you cannot sleep.

This is not how my life is supposed to be.

How can this be God's plan?

When will this end?

And maybe the weightiest question of all: *Why?*

But what if the frustration itself is the answer we seek? What if we could reframe this difficult season so that we see it not as something God is allowing to happen *to* us but *for* us? What if we chose an entirely different way of dealing with our frustration?

When we are tired of trying, there is nothing left to do but to get real with God about where we are and how we are feeling. Allow me to let you in on a little secret: God already knows anyway. God isn't surprised by our indignation. He isn't put off by our pity parties or our shouts to heaven that we're giving up. God cannot be anything but faithful to us. It's okay to admit our weakness and our frustrations. In fact, it's absolutely necessary.

Since the beginning of time, God has been dealing with people just like us who are flawed, insecure, and sinful. That is exactly why He sent Jesus to be for us what we never could be for ourselves.

Friend, maybe you are tired of trying because God wants you to recognize you don't need to keep trying. Instead of trying to fix things by being strong enough, good enough, and smart enough, God wants you to stop relying on yourself and your own efforts. Maybe tired of trying is exactly where God needs you to be because it's the only way to get you to face whatever it is you're trying very hard not to face.

God wants us to trust Him enough to let Him deal with whatever it is we're avoiding. He already knows what it is anyway. But just as Jacob was terrified of having to face Esau, we are scared to death of what the outcome of facing these things with God might be. We are

Friend, maybe you are tired of trying because God wants you to recognize you don't need to keep trying.

looking for any way out or around, but when God comes to bring true change in our lives, the only way out is through. God has a plan, and it is always for our good. But He must first reveal to us what is buried beneath our fears, and that revelation often comes through times of testing.

THE HIDDEN BENEFIT OF FRUSTRATION

According to James, the testing of our faith, those moments when frustration is all-consuming, actually produces something good in us: steadfastness. "Count it all joy," he writes, "when you meet trials of various kinds, for you know that the testing of your faith produces steadfastness" (James 1:2-3).

Here's a definition of what it means to be steadfast:

1. a: firmly fixed in place: IMMOVABLE
   b: not subject to change
2. firm in belief, determination, or adherence: LOYAL[3]

When we encounter seasons of frustration or testing, we must remember that it is not for nothing. The struggle has a purpose. It produces something in us that is immovable, firm, determined, and loyal. In a world where we can be knocked off our feet by the wind of every thought and opinion—y'all, we need this!

James goes on to write, "Let steadfastness have its *full effect*, that you may be perfect and complete, *lacking in nothing*" (James 1:4, emphasis added). To understand the full effect, we need to understand what James means by *lacking in nothing*.

Many of us believe God allows only the good, the blessed, and the best in our lives. And by that, we mean the easy, the happy, and the preferred. But even if that were true, let's be clear about what constitutes the good, the blessed, and the best from God's perspective. I would argue that the best things for us aren't necessarily the easiest things, but instead the deep internal work that often goes beyond our immediate understanding. God uses seasons of frustration to produce something good in us: making us more like Christ. That is what it means to be "perfect and complete, lacking in nothing."

Why is it so important to know what is fueling your frustration and to be able to define your disappointments with God? Two reasons—for your own sake and for the sake of others.

Defining Frustration for Your Own Sake

When you define your frustration, you take your first step toward the wrestle—the issue God wants you to face with Him. The dictionary defines frustration as "a deep chronic sense or state of insecurity and dissatisfaction arising from unresolved problems or unfulfilled needs."[4] Let's unpack that.

When you slow down and really dig into the emotions you're walking through now, it may hit you right between the eyes—it's not a shallow irritation but a deep sense of insecurity or dissatisfaction in the pit of your soul. It's an unfulfilled need that makes you question your core beliefs and rocks your trust in a good God. And it's not just any passing feeling but a chronic one.

If you had to put words to it, what is it you feel most insecure about or dissatisfied with right now? Sit with that insecurity or dissatisfaction for a moment. This is likely the core issue that is making you tired of trying. It's probably the reason you feel exposed, your deepest fears naked for all to gawk at, and why you're quickly losing the control you've tried so hard to maintain, perhaps for years. What are the unresolved problems in your life at the moment? What about unfulfilled needs?

There is such a temptation to rush past questions like these to get to the "answers," but I think any good counselor or therapist would agree with me that the answers may not end up being as important as the questions we need to ask ourselves about why we feel frustrated to begin with. The world is so fast paced, and we are desperate for quick solutions to make our problems disappear; but that is not how wrestling works. We have to be brave enough to hold on to God and look at the things we have been running from.

Feeling tired of trying doesn't come from a lack of potential solutions, but a lack of allowing ourselves to face the roots of our frustration and the roots of the pain that cause our exhaustion. To recognize the wrestling seasons in our lives, we have to be willing to look beyond the symptoms—our frustrations—to the cause. If we skip this step, we won't understand why the wrestle is necessary in the first place. Plus, our willingness to do that—to be honest about our struggles—is the testimony we can share with the world about what walking with Christ really looks like. With our lives, we demonstrate that it's possible to be both flawed and unconditionally loved.

> **F**eeling tired of trying doesn't come from a lack of potential solutions, but a lack of allowing ourselves to face the roots of our frustration and the roots of the pain that cause our exhaustion.

Defining Frustration for the Sake of Others

Imagine for a minute a world in which Christians never get to the place where they are willing to face the hardest things that come into their lives. Instead, they run from anything that smells of hard work or suffering. In addition to refusing to walk the same path that our Savior walked, we would have nothing to offer the world. What kind of faith is a faith we preach about and yet refuse to live ourselves? What kind of message would we be sending to the world if we call ourselves disciples and yet refuse to live up to the name?

The reason we must face the cause of our frustration, must recognize it, must engage in what God is inviting us to, no matter how bad it hurts, isn't just for you or me; it's also for a world that desperately needs to know that what we believe is not only our theology but our reality—that it is in fact possible to be "more than conquerors" (Romans 8:37). People who are watching how we live for Christ and follow Him need to see how the words we read in Scripture are the power for life in all circumstances, especially the hard ones. We are called to be living testimonies for others, even when we crawl through the most painful seasons of our lives. Others see us struggling, just as they do, but not without hope.

God is not asking us to walk through hard seasons merely for this purpose, but we must remember that our comfort is not the point. We must believe, by faith, that even when God says no or delays answers, He is still loving us best.

Does it make hard seasons any easier? No.

Does it mean they hurt less? No.

Does it mean we understand? No.

But it can help us discover a purpose in the pain, to learn how to wait on and trust in God, and to be steadfast, as the apostle James wrote, until we have a story of His faithfulness to tell. And friend, I am confident your life is already filled with stories of God's faithfulness. This is simply your next story being written.

FRUSTRATION THAT LEADS TO FREEDOM

Our chronic frustration is an indicator that something is wrong, that something needs to be addressed, and that somewhere along the way, we have shifted our focus from God to our own efforts. And so, God allows us to get to the end of ourselves, to become so tired of trying that we finally acknowledge we can get only so far with our own plans and our own strength. He does this not as punishment but to lead us to freedom that comes from letting go.

I didn't want to be broken or not okay. I wanted my life to look exactly as it always had, allowing me to feel comfortable and in control. It wasn't until I defined my frustration that I was finally able to admit I felt let down by God. And once I was willing to face that, God and I slowly began to move forward.

I leapt out of the car on that cold October day because I wanted to run and cry. People in the movies do things like that all the time, right? Perhaps my idealistic, slightly overdramatic self imagined a romantic scene in which I could bawl while my hair elegantly flowed behind me as I exited the car in a ballerina-esque, slow-motion leap. But let's be honest, the reality was much less romantic.

Just as I couldn't physically run and cry, we can't run and cry in our spiritual and emotional lives. And maybe that's part of why we're so frustrated—because we want to keep running but we can't. The wrestle God invites us to requires slowing down to face some things— and that takes time. We can't keep going because this isn't a time for running; it's a time to process our tears with God as we wrestle.

WHEN GOD HURTS YOUR FEELINGS

There is no normal life that is free of pain.
It's the very wrestling with our problems
that can be the impetus for our growth.

FRED ROGERS,
The World According to Mister Rogers

MY BREAKDOWN IN THE CAR THAT OCTOBER DAY was a cry for help, but as the months passed and my struggle continued, it faded into the background and not much changed in my life. Instead, I kept moving forward the best I knew how while being a wife and a mom. I couldn't stop the rest of my life just because I was in a wrestle. I had to wrestle in the midst of it—which is what I was doing one morning when my three-year-old sat on my lap singing, "Jesus loves me this I know, for the Bible tells me so." Tears streamed down my face, and I couldn't help but wonder, *Lord, do you love me? Because it just doesn't feel like it right now.*

I had been in our bedroom for the past hour contemplating, again, why the pain I was experiencing was happening. *Why me, why this, why now? Why?* It just didn't seem fair. I loathed myself for not being able to change. *What is wrong with me? Why can't I just feel better, do better, get over it, and be who I think I'm supposed to be?*

I was so used to what had worked previously in my life. I was used to having the strength, faith, and answers to pull myself through. I believed weakness was a flaw I could not afford to have. What did it say about me? What would happen if this didn't change? Hopelessness was a feeling I had become more and more familiar with. I pushed God away because I believed He was ashamed of me as well.

The boxes I had once loved to check as validation that I was okay no longer provided validation. Instead, they mocked me for not being enough and for not doing things right. I didn't have a godly attitude, I wasn't spending time with God praying or reading His Word, I could barely get my family to church, and maybe worst of all, I didn't care.

I wanted to sob.

I wanted to understand.

I wanted someone to get me out of this.

If hope were something I had to work for, then I was done.

The religious side of my brain did not approve: *Well, that's not very godly of you. Everyone, including God, is annoyed with your constant failure.* I didn't want to be ostracized or rejected from the church I had always been a part of, but I could no longer pretend I wasn't struggling or as desperate as I was.

God had hurt my feelings.

I thought we had a deal. I would do my part—obey, serve, spend time with Him—and then He would give me what I prayed for. Not houses, not cars, not to be a millionaire, but the simple things, like relief from being crushed by my own mind, income to pay our bills, my husband having a job where he could be home to help with the kids, and not believing that everyone hated me and there was no point to my life. These were things I believed I needed with all my heart.

WHEN GOD'S LOVE HURTS

What do we do in these seasons of our lives when God doesn't seem to be doing the things we think He should or acting the way we expect Him to? When we come to know God and walk closely with Him during difficult seasons, we learn how to hear His voice and take steps of faith, and we watch Him move in extraordinary ways in our lives. Throughout these experiences, we develop intimacy with God, and the fire of our love for Him burns so deep that we are sure nothing could ever extinguish it. We are committed to walking with Him day in and day out.

Then something happens. Suddenly or over time, God no longer feels close, and we can't help but ask, "Lord, don't you remember me? Why are you allowing this?" And it's in those moments that we begin to wonder, *Did I do something that caused God to take a step back? Why else would the God I have loved for so long ignore me?* So we take a step back in response, rejecting the God we feel has rejected us because we don't understand His silence. Instead of giving Him access to our bleeding and broken hearts, we try to keep ourselves safe. We don't know how to relate to this silent God, or we wonder if it's safe to seek Him when we're afraid to acknowledge how hurt we feel by His inaction.

We keep going through the motions of going to church, but we secretly resent every person who casually asks, "How are you?" We paste on a smile and reply, "Good" or "Fine," and keep walking. And yet, we long for someone to really want to know how we are. Because the truth is, we're not good and we're not fine. We are desperate to be saved out of this place that God has asked us to walk through.

Maybe part of feeling tired of trying is that on some level, we believe we have to try in order to be loved. When there is no strength left and we feel like a broken mess, we wonder what there could possibly be about us that God would want. We don't want to live like this, and other people seem to be overwhelmed by the broken record of pain that has become our lives, so we just assume God feels the same way.

Our souls can't help but cry out, "How is this love? How can this be the way God wants my life to be?"

Standing with empty hands and nothing but broken pieces of our former selves, we have important questions that need to be answered:

Does anyone see me?

Am I valuable?

Am I worthy?

Does anyone really love me, unconditionally?

And we're scared to death that the answer to all those questions is "No!" But we keep asking because we are made to seek answers. We ask our families, our friends, our churches, our leaders, and even social media. We perform for validation—for love—by trying harder, saying the right things, and playing the parts that have always brought the applause and approval our souls crave. But even when the people in our lives try to answer these questions for us, the answers never seem to be enough to make us feel seen, valuable, worthy, and loved. Every attempt slips quickly through our needy souls like sand in a sieve. God is the only one who can answer our questions and give us the validation we seek, but we're not always on speaking terms with God when we feel like He has hurt our feelings.

Even so, that doesn't keep God from trying to get through to us.

"Jesus loves me this I know, for the Bible tells me so." These simple words sung by a child who had no clue what was going on in my head became the whispers of the Lord to me in that moment.

God knows we don't understand, but He never stops loving us, even when we can't hear Him or we choose not to believe Him. Our ability to receive the love of God is not a prerequisite for Him loving us. When we are brave enough to be still, God breaks through our self-protective walls and speaks truth into our disappointment with Him. His whispers are tender and faithful.

> **Our ability to receive the love of God is not a prerequisite for Him loving us.**

"Jesus loves me this I know, for the Bible tells me so. Little ones to Him belong; they are weak, but He is strong."

Jesus loves me.

Jesus loves you.

Not because we can do the right things, not because we have so much to offer to Him, not because we've earned it, but because we are His children. We can be sure of this love because the Bible tells us it is so.

When we are children, we understand things in simple terms. When we become adults, we need to have answers to complex questions—we need to understand why, and we need to find solutions. But sometimes the only answer we get from God is an affirmation of His unfailing love.

"Yes, Jesus loves me! Yes, Jesus loves me! Yes, Jesus loves me! The Bible tells me so."

Maybe you have been singing this song and songs like it to the God you love and have served for years. I can't help but wonder if that is why what you are walking through hurts as much as it does. This same God you have loved, trusted, obeyed, and followed for all this time seems to have forgotten about you, your deep pain, and your desperation for a miracle—or the crushing weight of having to live without one.

God has hurt your feelings.

Logically and theologically, we know God does not intentionally hurt our feelings or do anything with malicious intent, but as C. S. Lewis once said, "We are not necessarily doubting that God will do the best for us; we are wondering how painful the best will turn out to be."[1]

In God's sovereignty, He sometimes allows things to happen in our lives that don't make any sense. Even though we trust God, we wrestle when we don't understand why He doesn't come through like we believe He should. When you love someone and that person lets you down, it hurts. It's as simple as that.

JACOB'S DISAPPOINTMENT WITH GOD

Jacob certainly had his own disappointments with God, times that made him mutter, "This is not the way my life was supposed to go." Picking up where we left off with his story, Jacob had just cheated his brother out of his birthright and deceived his father to obtain Esau's blessing. Esau was now determined to kill Jacob. Since God had promised to bless him, Jacob must have wondered how a death threat could possibly be the outcome of his attempt to be blessed. He had secured a double portion of the inheritance and all the rights of the firstborn, and yet he had to flee for his life? This was definitely not the way things were supposed to go.

When Rebekah caught wind of Esau's threats, she immediately sent Jacob to her brother's home far away to protect Jacob's life. On his way to his new home, God met him in a dream. You may have heard this part of Jacob's story referred to as "Jacob's Ladder." In the dream, Jacob saw angels ascending and descending into heaven on a ladder. God used the dream to once again confirm the plan and blessing He had for Jacob. Without a word of condemnation for his trickery or cheating, the Lord promised to bring Jacob home again and to bless him (Genesis 28:13-15).

Soon after, Jacob joined his mother's family and fell deeply in love with a woman named Rachel. To have her as his bride, he promised to work seven years for her father, Laban. But after Jacob completed his work, Laban tricked him and instead married him to Rachel's sister Leah. Once again, this was not the way things were supposed to go! How could this be part of the blessing God had promised him in the dream?

Jacob then worked another seven years to marry Rachel as well. Throughout this time, Laban continually tried to outwit Jacob and trick him, not only with his daughters, but also with the livestock Jacob managed for his father-in-law. Even so, Jacob had his own ways of subverting Laban's trickery and managed to turn things to his advantage. But Jacob's prosperity created resentment among Laban and his sons, and "Jacob saw that Laban did not regard him with favor as before" (Genesis 31:2).

After two decades of this, Jacob was surely at his wits' end. After trying so hard to make the best of a bad situation, this was his reward? But that's when God met Jacob again and said to him, "Return to the land of your fathers and to your kindred, and I will be with you" (Genesis 31:3). Surely disappointment with this entire scenario now weighed heavily on Jacob, and he wanted out as soon as possible. So he once again relied on deception to get what he wanted, this time by not telling Laban he intended to leave. He waited until Laban had gone to shear his sheep, and then Jacob packed up and left with all his family, possessions, and livestock.

When our expectations of how we think God should come through for us don't come close to what we are experiencing in our lives, it hurts.

Jacob may have succeeded in avoiding a confrontation with Laban, but he was now caught between two men he had deceived. There was fear behind him, because he was running from Laban, and fear ahead of him, as he would soon have to face Esau, the brother who wanted him dead.

For two decades, Jacob experienced disappointment after disappointment. God had promised a blessing, but nothing was playing out the way Jacob expected. When our expectations of how we think God should come through for us don't come close to what we are experiencing in our lives, it hurts.

THE HURT OF UNMET EXPECTATIONS

Most of us have had our feelings hurt many times over the years, but what do we do when it feels like God has hurt our feelings? And why does it hurt so bad? These are questions of the wrestle, and both require living in the uncomfortable space between our high expectations of God and our unwelcome realities with God. It hurts because our unmet expectations reveal our sense of entitlement—our belief that we have a right to expect certain things from God. And it hurts because we equate love only with things that feel good.

It Hurts Because of Expectations and Entitlement

Much of the wrestle I had was about letting go of my entitlement—my belief that, on some level, God owed me certain things. It's hard to admit that, but I'm guessing I'm not alone in this struggle. When we see our relationship with the God of the universe as transactional—as an exchange of one thing for another—we are deeply disappointed when things don't work out the way we think they should.

As I faced this disappointment and my own hurt feelings, I began to see how my relationship with God was wrapped tightly around what I assumed He would do for me. I had committed my life to serving Him and doing the right things, but I wasn't experiencing all the blessings I thought were owed me. After years of trusting God and asking him to lead me and help me grow, I hit a season in which nothing made sense. I was standing toe-to-toe with His sovereignty, and I no longer felt so sure about who God was. *What do I do with a God who allows things that cause me pain?* I was taken aback and faced with the reality that maybe this was not a God I wanted to be in a relationship with after all.

When we don't get what we feel we have a right to expect from God, our feelings will not be ignored. They demand to be heard and cause us to cry out, "No! This is not fair!" And what we usually mean by that is, "If I were God, this is not how I would have done it. I know what love is. I know what is right—and this is not it." Underneath it all, we think we know better than God and that He has missed the mark entirely.

Maybe even reading those words makes you squirm or feel uncomfortable. It made me uncomfortable writing it. We can believe something logically, but it is only when we no longer measure up to our own expectations and are tired of trying altogether that we are faced with the reality of our beliefs. Maybe what we really want is a small *g* god—a god created in our own image, a god we understand, a god within our control.

It was only when I allowed myself to express my disappointment with God that He gently revealed the truth—my hope had never fully been in Him. Instead, my hope was in my perceived ability to control things so they worked out the way I thought they should. That's when I had to face hard questions:

Do I love and trust God only when He does what I think He should?

Do I love God for Himself alone, or only when He answers yes to my requests?

As much as it might hurt to hear, I think deep down we all know that God's number one goal in our lives is not to give us what we want, but to make us more like Christ. And one of the ways that happens is when we make choices that aren't always easy.

Forgiving when we want to hold on to bitterness and resentment.

Walking by faith and not by our feelings.

Loving people, even when we might not like them.

Laying down our rights so we can take up God's righteousness.

It's not an easy truth to accept, and it feels especially harsh when we can't see how the hard season we are walking through could possibly be God's best for us. But in the middle of the pain of a no from God, it helps to remember someone else who had to endure the pain of a no.

Jesus wrestled too. Do you remember what the Bible says about His experiences in Gethsemane? Jesus wrestled with God to the point that He sweat drops of blood (Luke 22:44). He cried out, saying, "Father, if you are willing, remove this cup from me. Nevertheless, not my will, but yours, be done" (Luke 22:42). But God's answer to Jesus' plea was no. God was not willing to remove the cup from Jesus, His own precious Son, even though He could have.

If you have been wondering whether God's no to you means He just doesn't love you as much as He loves others, let that lie go. God loved His perfect Son more than we could ever comprehend, but that didn't stop God from saying no to Jesus' prayer. God doesn't say no because He is mean, because of our wrong behaviors, or because there is something disappointing about us. He says no because there is a purpose He can't accomplish any other way. Although it's tempting to assess God's love by the degree to which His will aligns with our will, God's ways are not our ways, and they won't always make sense to us. Trusting Him and following Him even when we don't understand is the definition of living by faith.

It's only on the other side of God's devastating no to Jesus that we see clearly what could never have been accomplished without it. Jesus' purpose was to reconcile us to God through His death and resurrection. That's what would have been lost if God had prioritized Jesus' rescue from the cross over the purpose His death and resurrection would fulfill. But I doubt knowing there was a purpose behind it made God's will any less painful for Jesus. He still experienced the terror, loneliness, desperation, and weight of it all.

I take heart in the fact that God didn't reprimand Jesus for asking to be saved from the pain, nor did God minimize what Jesus was suffering. When we are suffering, God doesn't think less of us for asking to be rescued, nor does He invalidate our pain. The Lord cares about all of that, but He also has a purpose for us. That means there will come a point when we have to make a choice, just as Jesus did. Will we dare to love and trust God even when His answer is no? Will we trust He is a God who loves us and knows what He is doing even when we are walking through the hardest days of our lives?

Will we dare to love and trust God even when His answer is no?

Jesus chose to trust, to surrender. "Nevertheless, not my will, but yours, be done."

No one can make this choice for us, we must decide. And sometimes the only way to make that decision is to wrestle through it. Remember, even Jesus wrestled as He prayed to a God who required what seemed too much of Him.

For us, too, this is where the wrestle is required. When we begin to see that we have unmet expectations of God and a sense of entitlement, we can choose to whisper in faith, "Help me, Lord. Not my will, but yours, be done."

It Hurts Because We Equate Love Only with Things That Feel Good

Love is supposed to feel good, and so when God hurts our feelings, it doesn't make sense. But we don't have to look any further than the relationship we have with our own children to know that our love doesn't always feel good to them. Sometimes we have to make choices that they don't understand or that feel painful to them in the short term because we know that is what's best for them in the long term. God, the best and first Father, does the same for us.

When my youngest son was a baby, he never wanted to sleep. Now that he's nine years old and I know more about his personality, I think he was afraid he was going to miss out on something. But after a certain amount of time of refusing sleep, he would cry uncontrollably. When he reached that point, I would tuck his little body close to mine and rock him while holding him tightly. He did his best to fight me with everything he had. He looked up at me with tears in his eyes and a quivering bottom lip that asked, *Why, Mommy?* Holding him tightly felt like punishment and frustration to him. It definitely was not what he wanted, but it was what he needed. He didn't know he needed it, but I did. I teared up looking into his exhausted eyes because I knew he didn't understand why I wouldn't let him have his way. But love does what is best for the beloved.

Sometimes it hurts when God does what is best for us, and it can be tempting to keep our distance from Him. But the truth is, in most cases, we know He has been faithful in our lives up to this point, and our hearts ache for Him. We don't understand how this could be best for us, especially when we are grieving what we believe He could have done and yet chose not to do for some sovereign reason.

THE BLESSING OF TRUSTING GOD WHEN HE SAYS NO

If anyone knew the pain of an unmet expectation and might have wondered how it could be loving, it would be John the Baptist. John was Jesus' cousin, and he had dedicated his life to knowing God, following God, and preparing the way for Jesus' ministry on earth. John was known for his boldness in preaching the truth, for calling people to repentance, and for radically living out God's call on his life. And it was this commitment to his calling—to speaking the truth without apology—that landed him in prison and ultimately cost him his life.

What must John have been thinking when he ended up in prison? He had done everything God had called him to do. If nothing else, it seems reasonable to assume he felt deeply disappointed in how things were turning out. This, of all things, was not how he saw his ministry going.

Up to that point, the future had seemed promising. Jesus had come on the scene and was performing miracles. John had baptized Jesus and had seen the Holy Spirit descend on Him with his very own eyes. That must have filled his heart with wonder and hope. For years, John had wandered in the wilderness, dedicating his life to preparing for *this* moment. Finally, the Messiah had come! Jesus, the King of kings and Lord of lords had come to fulfill what God's people had been reading about and anticipating for generations!

John and many other followers of Jesus had expectations of what the Messiah would look like. John likely had a vision of how he thought things would go, what this new kingdom would look like, and how Jesus would act. If Jesus could use His power for anyone, wouldn't it be for John, who had played a vital role in preparing people for His ministry—not to mention the fact that he and Jesus were cousins?

We catch a glimpse of what was plaguing John's mind when he sent his disciples to ask Jesus a question: "Are you the one who is to come, or shall we look for another?" (Matthew 11:3). And there are several other questions anyone in John's position might have asked as well.

Do you not know where I am and what's happening to me?

Is this right?

Is this part of the plan?

Are you not going to save me?

Jesus replied, "Go and tell John what you hear and see: the blind receive their sight and the lame walk, lepers are cleansed and the deaf hear, and the dead are raised up, and the poor have good news preached to them" (Matthew 11:4-5). In other words, "Yes, I am the one."

Jesus' response was to assure John that, despite where he found himself, the mission was being fulfilled. God's purpose was being realized even though John and others wrestled with the way it was coming about.

Then Jesus added this curious statement: "And blessed is the one who is not offended by me" (Matthew 11:6). What did Jesus mean by that?

Like many Jews of his day, John expected the Messiah to come in power, establish an earthly kingdom, and declare exactly who He was. While Jesus affirmed who He was, He didn't meet John's expectations of the Messiah. And Jesus' response acknowledged John's wrestle at finding himself in the uncomfortable space between high expectations and unwelcome reality. Jesus invited John to have faith, to trust that He was who He said He was, even when things weren't turning out as John had expected. John's only alternative was to take offense and reject Jesus.

Jesus understood that John might feel hurt or even betrayed when He didn't intervene to rescue him from prison. Jesus also knew that there would be times we might feel hurt by His lack of action in our lives—that we might take offense and be tempted to look elsewhere for a savior when He doesn't rescue us as we expect. But He gives us the same promise He gave to John—that He is who He says He is. And when our high expectations crash into an unwelcome reality, He invites us to have faith—to not let our unmet expectations become a stumbling block to our relationship with Him.

We are blessed when we are not offended by the ways of God.

WHAT TO DO WHEN IT SEEMS GOD HAS HURT YOUR FEELINGS

So what do we do when we feel like God has hurt our feelings? We find ways to hold on to faith while we navigate the frustrating space between our expectations and our reality. In the midst of my own choice to wrestle, I eventually learned three lessons that helped me hold on to faith—I needed to let myself feel, to recognize my progress, and to surround myself with support.

1. Let Yourself Feel

It's okay that you are battling difficult feelings about God. God hasn't rejected you. He loves you. He wants you to trust Him and to hold on for the beautiful blessings that are still on their way, even if trusting and holding on feel difficult right now.

God made you, and He understands what it is to struggle and

hurt. That's why He sent Jesus. The prophet Isaiah said the Messiah would be sent "to bring good news to the poor . . . to bind up the brokenhearted, to proclaim liberty to the captives, and the opening of the prison to those who are bound; to proclaim the year of the LORD's favor, and the day of vengeance of our God; to comfort all who mourn; to grant to those who mourn in Zion—to give them a beautiful headdress instead of ashes, the oil of gladness instead of mourning" (Isaiah 61:1-3).

When we feel as though God has hurt our feelings, we must be brave enough to take that hurt to Him, to face Him with our pain so He can give us beauty for our ashes.

God knew we would be brokenhearted, prisoners to our pain, in need of comfort in our mourning, and in need of hope when we are sitting in the ashes of loss and disappointment. When we feel as though God has hurt our feelings, we must be brave enough to take that hurt to Him, to face Him with our pain so He can give us beauty for our ashes.

Avoidance, denial, walls of self-protection, and apathy are all ways of not feeling, of denying the deep wounds we carry. Telling ourselves to push past the pain or ignore it only deepens the wound and prolongs our suffering. To make it through the wrestle, we have to let ourselves feel the pain.

What does God's Word teach us about how to let ourselves feel, to deal with our feelings? Here are three principles:

We can be honest with God. One of the things I love most about the Psalms is how honest they are about how hard life can be. Consider this psalm written by David:

> I am weary with my moaning;
>> every night I flood my bed with tears;

I drench my couch with my weeping.
My eye wastes away because of grief;
    it grows weak because of all my foes.
Depart from me, all you workers of evil,
    for the LORD has heard the sound of my weeping.
The LORD has heard my plea;
    the LORD accepts my prayer.

PSALM 6:6-9

Not only is David honest about how deeply grieved he is, he also affirms that God has heard his pleas and accepted his prayer. When we are honest with God, we can rely on the promise that He listens and accepts us as we are. There is no reason to hide, minimize, or sugarcoat how we're really feeling.

We can complain to God. When I'm struggling, nothing encourages me more than to see examples of others in God's Word who bring their complaints to God. Here's another example from a psalm written by David:

With my voice I cry out to the LORD;
    with my voice I plead for mercy to the LORD.
I pour out my complaint before him;
    I tell my trouble before him.

PSALM 142:1-2

David doesn't hold back or try to hide his feelings from God, but boldly pours them out before Him. We can do the same because God already knows how we feel, and He longs to be with us in our troubles.

We can express our pain to God while still remembering God's faithfulness. There is a way that we can be honest with God and at the same time remind ourselves who He is and what He is capable of. We have a beautiful example of this from the prophet Jeremiah.

> So I say, "My endurance has perished;
>> so has my hope from the LORD."
>
> Remember my affliction and my wanderings,
>> the wormwood and the gall!
> My soul continually remembers it
>> and is bowed down within me.
> But this I call to mind,
>> and therefore I have hope:
>
> The steadfast love of the LORD never ceases;
>> his mercies never come to an end;
> they are new every morning;
>> great is your faithfulness.
> "The LORD is my portion," says my soul,
>> "therefore I will hope in him."
>
> The LORD is good to those who wait for him,
>> to the soul who seeks him.
> LAMENTATIONS 3:18-26

As Jeremiah did, we can bring our doubts and laments to God, and in the same breath, we can also affirm that God is good, God is faithful, and God will be good to us again!

God is not surprised by our hurt feelings, doubts, frustrations, or disappointments with Him. He doesn't want us to deny our pain but to invite Him into our pain. He wants to be with us in the wrestle so He can do the work He has intended all along. Are you willing to let yourself feel and to allow God to meet you in your pain?

2. Recognize Your Progress

Even when you are tired of trying, spiraling into discouragement, or giving voice to your disappointment, you are still taking steps toward progress. The fact that you are feeling these painful emotions is an indicator that something much deeper needs to be acknowledged and addressed. There is no drive-through window for breakthrough, so be kind to yourself as you begin to face what God wants to change. Every choice to trust Him is another step forward, and every step matters.

> Every choice to trust Him is another step forward, and every step matters.

Wrestling is not easy; it is not fast; it is not a box quickly checked so you can move on. There will be days you make mistakes, days you doubt, and days you fall down and feel like staying down. When that happens, remember that how you feel in that moment is not how you will feel forever. It will pass, and you will see light again. And when you feel like you have made no progress, remind yourself of all the ways you have chosen to take a step of faith, however small, to trust God again. To recognize your forward movement is to acknowledge that this is a place you are passing through, not a place where you are setting up permanent residence. There's nothing to be gained by being harsh with yourself, so let yourself off the hook for not doing everything perfectly. Keep reminding yourself that even when you are not yet where you want to be, you are still far from where you used to be.

It's okay to recognize your progress, to have a mindset of affirmation rather than negation. Here's a pro tip I picked up about the importance of mindset. When Team USA wrestling coaches were asked what makes a great wrestler, one coach said, "The best wrestlers . . . look at every experience as a positive one that can make them better because of it."[2]

You, my friend, are becoming a great wrestler. In every round, perhaps the most impactful thing you can do is to make the hard choice again and again to shift your mindset. Just as the great wrestlers do, you can look for what you are learning, affirm how it is making you better, and recognize your progress. That's how you reframe the experience to bring you strength rather than defeat.

Recognizing your progress might take practice, especially if you have developed a habit of focusing only on how weak you feel or how far you have to go. But remember this promise God gave to Jacob in his dream: "Behold, I am with you and will keep you wherever you go, and will bring you back to this land. For I will not leave you until I have done what I have promised you" (Genesis 28:15).

When the road is long and the wrestle intense, we know that God is using this for our good, and He will get us where He wants us to be if we will continue to hang on.

3. Surround Yourself with Support

When you are in a wrestling season and struggling with disappointment with God, it's more important than ever to surround yourself with other believers who will support you and remind you of who God is. You need people who can have faith on your behalf and who can speak faith over your life. Inviting others into your wrestle might not feel like something you want to do—or even like you are able to do—but it is vital for wrestling well.

In our hardest seasons, we are driven to protect ourselves, and sometimes we think that means isolating and pushing people away.

The enemy will often convince us that others don't understand or don't care, and that we must wrestle on our own. But refusing to believe this lie is also part of the wrestle. And believe me, as an introvert, I know how hard inviting others into the wrestle can be. But I also learned the hard way that there's no substitute for the support and encouragement of others.

Here are two things you can do to surround yourself with a godly support community: Invite a few people to be your inner circle and immerse yourself in truth daily.

Invite a few people to be your inner circle. While opening up might feel scary, prayerfully ask the Lord to lead you to two or three people whom you can trust. Once you've invited those safe friends to be your inner circle, ask them to check in with you weekly or biweekly. Give them permission to ask you how you are—how you *really* are. It is easy to answer "fine" to this question when you are anything but fine. You need to allow trustworthy people into your business, because they care, and they want to help you shoulder the burden.

Ask them to pray for you. You don't have to share all the details if you don't want to, but let them know how hard life is for you and that you are floundering. Your inner circle can't support you if they don't know how badly you need it. Prayer is vitally important as God leads you to the deeper work He wants to do in you. When your close friends check in with you weekly or biweekly, tell them what you're battling so they can pray for those things. In addition to feeling the power of their support and prayers, sharing your struggles will also help you be more aware of what you are working through and recognize the progress you're making.

Give your trusted inner circle permission to speak biblical wisdom into your life. This is vital when you get stuck in your own negative thinking and patterns of behavior. You need spiritually mature friends to remind you of what is true about who God is and who you are.

While the people we surround ourselves with are far from perfect, the Lord often uses them to help us experience His love in our hardest seasons. Most likely, those in your inner circle have been through wrestling seasons themselves and walked away changed. Lean on their experience and faith to help you remember that God is always faithful. It matters which voices we listen to most.

Immerse yourself in truth daily. When we're in the middle of a wrestle, we are especially vulnerable to distorted thinking and lies. And when those lies go unchallenged, we can easily lose our way, lose our hope, or fall into bitterness. You guard your heart when you saturate it with teaching, worship, and messages that remind you of what is true, despite your feelings.

Especially at the beginning of my wrestle, I found it hard to read the Bible or have regular prayer and journaling time as I had in the past. Because I didn't have the strength for that, I had others speak the truth to me—daily. As I went about my daily chores, I listened to recorded sermons, audio books, and podcasts by Christian leaders and teachers and let them remind me of truth. I also listened to worship music. Immersing myself in truth in these ways helped me hold on to my faith until I had the strength to read the Bible and pray for myself again—and that day did come.

If you aren't sure where to start, ask your inner circle—the people you've allowed to speak wisdom into your life—to suggest authors, teachers, podcasters, and musicians they recommend. Choose resources that point you to Jesus as the answer, as He is the only answer.

God has equipped and called many people who love Jesus, love His Word, and have walked hard roads ahead of us. When we are weary or even unwilling, God enables others to serve us so we can still be immersed in truth even as we wrestle.

Let yourself feel, recognize your progress, and surround yourself with support. While these three steps will require a bit of thought and reaching out, they are vitally important. To wrestle well, we must be equipped. We have a long journey ahead of us, and we need these tools in our tool belt as we proceed.

CHOOSE TO TRUST A GOOD GOD

My depression was a result of not giving myself permission to wrestle with painful emotions. I kept telling myself I wasn't allowed to have them, they were wrong, and I was bad. But the more I denied how I felt, the more I postponed the grieving process that was necessary to move forward with the Lord. I also grew more and more resentful toward God because I told myself He didn't want to hear it—He would talk to me again, bless me again, use me again when I could get myself together. But it was only when I finally acknowledged how hurt I was, how unfair it felt, and asked Him why He was allowing this to happen to me—without judging myself for doing so—that I was able to receive from Him again.

Anything we refuse to admit or confess will remain toxic for us. We don't have to have our thoughts fully formed; we don't have to know the next steps to take; we don't even have to feel good about it; we just have to bring ourselves as we are to the foot of the cross and admit what's true. That's when we finally understand that God's grace is about so much more than just saving us from hell. We don't need grace just once at salvation; we need grace every day. That's the transforming grace that continues to change us. Sometimes that change looks like facing hardships we never imagined so we can experience God in ways we never could any other way. His grace does something in us we could never do on our own, both in our salvation from hell and in our salvation from our own brokenness.

When we are willing to confess how deeply hurt we feel that God has let us down, we accept God's invitation to the wrestle. He invites us to ask our questions—and to let Him ask His.

When God invites us to wrestle with Him, He is looking for our surrender—for our willingness to let Him do what He wants to do in our lives. If you're like me, surrender probably doesn't sound like something you want any part of. It sounds like weakness; it sounds like giving up control; it sounds like being beaten—and nobody wants that. But that's not what it means to surrender to God. In fact, it is the enemy who wants us to believe the lie that surrender to God is not for our benefit. When we acknowledge and surrender our weakness to God, we are not defeated but empowered. Remember God's promise? "My power is made perfect in weakness" (2 Corinthians 12:9).

When we give up control, we allow a God who is much wiser than us to be in charge. If we feel like we have been beaten, it may be that surrendering the compulsion to try so hard is what God is really after. He wants to be our source, our strength, our rescuer.

If you're wondering what surrendering to God looks like or are unsure where to start, here's a simple practice you can try: Fold your hands when you pray. The early Christians adopted this practice from the Romans, who viewed folded hands as a sign of submission. To fold one's hands was to acknowledge an authority and the person's choice to submit to that authority. Prisoners would assume this position, as is still common today, when having their hands tied or shackled.

When you clasp your hands together as you cry out to God, you are acknowledging your need to surrender. It is a way of saying, "You are God, and I am not," or as Jesus prayed, "Not my will, but yours, be done." Clasping your hands allows you to demonstrate physically the same posture of surrender you are offering to God with your heart. It is a reminder that you are choosing to trust a good God.

Surrender is a process, friend. Today, turn your heart just a little more toward the God you know loves you and ask for the grace that He is more than willing to give. Pray a simple prayer such as, "Lord, I don't know how, I don't have the strength, but I surrender because I trust you want what is best. Please give me the grace to face what you are trying to show me and

> When God hurts our feelings, part of the surrendering process requires standing with our Lord and grieving what He has chosen not to do.

to hold on to you until you bless me." And if you don't feel ready to pray that prayer, you might start with this one: "God, make me willing to be made willing."

When God hurts our feelings, part of the surrendering process requires standing with our Lord and grieving what He has chosen not to do. As we prepare our hearts to uncover the source of our pain and struggle, let's hold tight to Him as we next consider why God is leading us to wrestle.

WHEN GOD REVEALS UNHEALTHY ROOTS

Repeated actions are stored as habits. If the
repeated actions aren't fundamentally sound,
then what comes out in a game can't be sound.
What comes out will be bad habits.

CHUCK KNOX,
professional football coach

I GREW UP IN A DESERT. Imagine those scenes from old westerns with gigantic tumbleweeds blowing through nothingness, and you'll have a pretty good picture of the backdrop for my childhood. Needless to say, we had a lot of weeds in our yard. And if my dad taught me anything about weeds, it's that you have to pull them out by the roots. You have to dig deep, grip firmly, and use all your strength—which sounds an awful lot like wrestling to me. If you don't take the time and trouble to dig them out by the roots, the weeds will be back in no time.

As the Lord began to help me identify my frustration and admit my feelings were hurt because I felt so disappointed with Him, it became clear He wanted to dig up some unhealthy roots in my life—things I could not or did not want to see up to that point.

I had spent many years trying to make the garden of my life look beautiful and presentable by hacking away at those weeds, but I only dealt with them at the surface. Soon, those ugly things were popping up yet again. I was caught up in unhealthy patterns and expectations that were keeping me stuck, but I couldn't see that. I just wanted people to do, be, and act the way I wanted them to so that my life could run more smoothly. Why wouldn't they just play the part I needed them to play in my life? Why wasn't God changing them to help me?

At the time, I still believed that I could get the answers I wanted and the relief I was desperate for by dealing with all these things on the surface, but little by little God began directing my attention to the roots—to the deeper patterns within me that He wanted to remove. If I'm honest, I was furious. I didn't want to look at my roots. I wanted to be healed. Once again, I had a hard choice to make—would I let God do what He had come to do? Would I trust Him even in what felt like a brutal process?

THE WRESTLE REVEALS WHAT WE'VE YET TO RECOGNIZE

When God meets us in our places of uprooting, He uses our hardships to reveal what it is we are really struggling with—the issues that we've yet to recognize or acknowledge. We want to take our gardening shears and snip away at what we can see, but to ignore the roots is to invite a bumper crop of weeds to choke out anything of beauty that has been planted in our lives. While we might be willing to take that chance, God refuses to leave us in our brokenness.

How many times in your life have you sensed the Lord calling you to address the roots of a problem in your life, but you chose to run from Him instead? The fear is that if you give God access to the roots you have long left buried, you may not be able to recover. You have been doing your best to keep these weeds at bay, which is part of what makes you so tired of trying. These roots often take the form of accusations—internal voices that tell you you've never been wanted, you will never measure up, people have never liked you, you deserve rejection, and you will always be overlooked. You are deeply terrified that you are, in fact, way too much but never enough.

These are the things we truly believe about ourselves. Never mind that we say all the right things about having our identity in Christ. When we are anchored by toxic roots, we don't really understand what it even means to have our identity in Christ. It sounds good, it sounds right, and we want it to be true. But we don't yet know how to truly live it. And until we know how to live it, we'll be at the mercy of all the accusations we have been harboring for years, scared to death we will be found out.

My friend, this is why we choose to wrestle.

We must enter this season of wrestling with God because it is the only way He can reveal to us the roots of the false identities we are living with and the lies we are believing.

The wrestle reveals what we have yet to recognize, and this was exactly what happened in Jacob's wrestle with God. If Jacob were here with us today, he might confirm that this was one of the most difficult aspects of his experience. Perhaps he would also point out how he was unaware of the patterns in his life, of tricking and being tricked, and that he was trying his very best to get from his family members what he felt was owed to him, even if it meant deceiving them. He had cheated his brother, Esau, to get the birthright and blessing, and he had schemed to flee from his father-in-law, taking away his daughters and grandchildren without his knowledge or blessing.

Frustration and fear led Jacob to the place in which he now found himself. Would his father-in-law pursue him and try to force him to return? Would Esau kill Jacob and his family on sight?

As Jacob made his way back to his homeland, he sent messengers ahead to Esau and anxiously gave them these instructions: "Thus you shall say to my lord Esau: Thus says your servant Jacob, 'I have sojourned with Laban and stayed until now. I have oxen, donkeys, flocks, male servants, and female servants. I have sent to tell my lord, in order that I may find favor in your sight'" (Genesis 32:4-5). Remember, Jacob was afraid for his life and for the lives of all who were with him. When he alerted Esau to all he had brought with him, I imagine it was Jacob's way of saying, "Look at me, look at what I have, look at what I have accomplished. Please accept me."

But when the messengers returned, all they had to say was, "We came to your brother Esau, and he is coming to meet you, and there are four hundred men with him" (Genesis 32:6).

It's not hard to imagine what Jacob must have felt in that moment—the palpable anxiety gripping his chest, the shortness of breath. What should he do? What could he do? The last thing he had ever heard from his brother was a death threat. But now he had so much more than just his own life to lose.

Jacob decided to break up his large caravan into two groups, with the idea that if Esau attacked the first group, the second one might be spared. Protect, strategize, and struggle for solutions—he was relying on what he had yet to recognize were his patterns of self-reliance.

We then read Jacob's first prayer recorded in God's Word.

> And Jacob said, "O God of my father Abraham and God of my father Isaac, O Lord who said to me, 'Return to your country and to your kindred, that I may do you good,' I am not worthy of the

least of all the deeds of steadfast love and all the faithfulness that you have shown to your servant, for with only my staff I crossed this Jordan, and now I have become two camps. Please deliver me from the hand of my brother, from the hand of Esau, *for I fear him*, that he may come and attack me, the mothers with the children. But you said, 'I will surely do you good, and make your offspring as the sand of the sea, which cannot be numbered for multitude.'"

GENESIS 32:9-12, emphasis added

Like Jacob, we can bring our desperation and fear-filled prayers to God as well. Often it is not until we are confronted with our fears that we are willing to look at our underlying patterns. When nothing we have tried is working, we can no longer rely on ourselves, and so we finally turn to God. And maybe getting us to this moment was always His purpose. God doesn't want to punish us for relying on ourselves or for our underlying patterns, He wants to set us free of them. This is our opportunity to acknowledge whatever it is that God is asking us to face and to confess that we have come to the end of ourselves. As Jacob did, we, too, can ask for deliverance and boldly remind God of what He has promised us in His Word.

> Often it is not until we are confronted with our fears that we are willing to look at our underlying patterns.

After crying out to God, Jacob sent servants ahead of him bearing gifts for his brother, Esau. After the servants, he sent his wives and his children along with everything else he had. That's when we read, "And Jacob was left alone. And a man wrestled with him until the breaking of the day" (Genesis 32:24).

God's immediate answer to Jacob's prayer was the wrestle. Let that sink in.

Jacob knew God had promised to do him good, but his high expectations of God's goodness were now face-to-face with an unwelcome reality—Esau and his four hundred men. When Jacob prayed for deliverance, God could have answered in any number of ways, but the answer He chose was to invite Jacob to wrestle.

Many times when we are afraid and desperate for rescue, God invites us to wrestle as an answer to our prayers. Gone are the days of trying to earn favor by proving our worth: "Look at me, look at what I have, look at what I have accomplished. Please accept me." No longer will He allow us to rely on our own strength, our own wisdom, our own schemes. This is when we realize all our go-to solutions to protect, strategize, and struggle for a way out are no longer working. This is when we wrestle.

God meets us in the wrestle to reveal what we don't yet recognize. So when we're struggling and don't know what to do, it helps to shift our focus from our frustration over what God *isn't* doing to what God *is* doing through the wrestle. We begin to do that when we look for the lessons, pay attention to what we're thinking, and move in grace.

LOOK FOR THE LESSONS

Why are we given tests in school? To see if we actually know the things we've been taught. We can sit in class and do the homework, but it's only when the test is given and we are under pressure that we demonstrate what we've learned.

God tests us in similar ways. He wants us to graduate to the next level of growth, but He must make us ready first, and He wants us to demonstrate what we've learned—not for His sake, but for ours. It is so easy to say that we believe something, that we trust God, that we walk by faith—until we are under pressure. That's when what is really in us comes out.

When you are under pressure, what comes out of you? Is there a discrepancy between what you have always claimed to believe and how you respond?

For me, that discrepancy often looked like saying I trusted God when, really, I trusted my friends and family. I wanted them to validate me and save me. On one particularly bad night during my depression, instead of demonstrating my trust in God, I demonstrated an unhealthy reliance on my family. That's what came out of me when I was under pressure.

I had stayed up all night thinking horrible thoughts. I imagined my family attending my funeral and how much they would regret not stepping in to do what I felt they should. Is that what it would take to get them to care? I was furious that the people who were supposed to support me and get me through this were keeping me at arm's length. I felt judged and rejected by them in my time of deepest need. So I decided to do something about it.

I sent all three of my siblings, their spouses, and my parents a group text, a belligerent text full of rage and frustration. It was my desperate attempt to get them to see how serious this was and to demand that they do something—anything—about it.

I waited for a response, but no response ever came. Not one of the eight people who could have reached out to me, did. I was devastated. It was glaring proof of what I had feared—that not even my own family cared what happened to me. I felt like I couldn't breathe. In my most desperate moment, I experienced what felt like the greatest betrayal and rejection of my life.

In the days that followed, I felt desperation rush over me. I couldn't talk to my family, so I put out a Facebook post asking for anyone who was available to chat with me. Three random friends volunteered their time, and I talked endlessly about the injustice and pain I was drowning in. One friend said bluntly, "Just forget them." It felt soothing to my angry and hurt soul, but I knew God didn't want me to forget my family. What God wanted me to forget or let go of was my expectation that my family could save me. Suddenly, God's message was clear. I knew the Lord was saying to me, "Ash, you already have a Savior, and it isn't your family." God had orchestrated this moment so He could reveal what I had yet to recognize—that I wanted them to be my savior.

Ouch.

The truth of that message hit me square between the eyes, and I learned the lesson. When I was under pressure, I wasn't turning to God for who I claimed He was—my Savior. Instead, I was angry at my family for failing to fulfill a role they were never meant to have in my life. I had to be willing to let them off the hook for not being able to save me.

Accepting God's invitation to the wrestle means choosing to bravely face all we have been running from.

This was a lesson I could not have learned if God had not allowed the pain to reveal what I had not yet recognized. And it was one of many other lessons I learned as I continued to hang on to God for dear life.

Accepting God's invitation to the wrestle means choosing to bravely face all we have been running from. When He reveals what we hadn't previously recognized, it's not to shame us or guilt us, but to set us free (Galatians 5:1).

PAY ATTENTION TO WHAT YOU'RE THINKING

Viktor Frankl was an Austrian neurologist, psychiatrist, and Holocaust survivor. In 1942, he and his family were sent to Nazi concentration camps where his parents, his brother, and his wife died. Frankl survived but suffered through three years in four camps. After the war, he reflected on his experiences in a book called *Man's Search for Meaning*. He wrote, "Everything can be taken from a man but one thing: the last of the human freedoms—to choose one's attitude in any given set of circumstances, to choose one's own way."[1] It's a powerful reminder that we always have a choice and that it's important to pay attention to what we're thinking.

As we consider our thoughts, we can choose to walk down the path in our minds that leads to bitterness and resentment, or with every ounce of strength we can muster, we can choose to believe that God is still good, and that God is not doing this *to* us but *for* us.

When my family did not text me back, I was at my lowest point. I was spiritually exhausted and so tired of trying. But it was only when I reached that point that I realized this was what God was intending all along. God had a purpose in allowing me to get to the end of all my trying, all my resources, all my plans, all my excuses, and even all my rescuers.

I sobbed with exhaustion, knowing that it was now just God and me, and then I began to feel the spiritual reality of what was happening. I had allowed my mind to be the dumping ground for every garbage lie the enemy tossed my way. And I believed each lie as if it were a certain truth for which I was constantly seeking evidence.

That's when I sensed God whispering a simple question in my spirit, "Have you had about enough?"

I had.

His response seemed to be, "Now, daughter, I am going to teach you how to fight back." In other words, my mind could no longer be the dumping ground for lies. It was time to put a stop to the battering thoughts that constantly beat me down. How? By paying attention to what I was thinking, one thought at a time.

The apostle Paul wrote, "We destroy arguments and every lofty opinion raised against the knowledge of God, and take every thought captive to obey Christ" (2 Corinthians 10:5). Every thought that comes into our minds can be measured against God's truth. Then we take captive every thought that does not obey Christ and His Word. We do not have to allow our minds to be the dumping grounds for lie-filled thoughts about ourselves, about others, and especially about God.

For years, I had read this verse about taking every thought captive and believed it to be true, but I had never applied it—not really. Yet once I began to put it into practice, little by little, thought by thought, day by day, God taught me how to take my thoughts captive. And believe me, some of them were wild and hard to catch after having had free rein of the place for so long. But I'd had enough, and God was teaching me how to fight back. I would no longer allow my thoughts to bully me in a place where Christ was already King. Not anymore.

You can declare "Not anymore" in your life too. I understand the mean thoughts you may have about yourself and even the ones you think about yourself on behalf of others. I understand the doubts and accusations you may have about God, and the ones you fear God has about you. I understand not because I know what flows through your mind, but because I have had, and still have, those same thoughts myself. The enemy has been lying to humanity for ages, but God is here, in this wrestle, teaching us how to fight for our minds.

Remember, the wrestle reveals what you don't yet recognize. As you hold on to the Lord during this process, pay attention to what you're thinking. God wants to help you fight back by replacing lies

WHEN GOD REVEALS UNHEALTHY ROOTS

and bad thinking patterns with His truth. He wants to set your mind free!

MOVE IN GRACE

As Christ-followers, we all have had the experience of realizing we are sinners in need of a Savior. We were overcome with the truth that Christ died to save us, something we could never do for ourselves. At that moment, we were in awe of grace, receiving what we didn't deserve and could never earn. We were thankful and wanted to commit our lives to a God who would do something so extraordinary for us.

But somewhere along the way, we came to believe that while it was grace that saved us, everything else that needed to change in our lives was all up to us. We knew we had to rely fully on Christ for salvation, but from there onward, we had to pull our own weight.

This, my friends, is one of the core reasons we are so tired of trying. We feel the weight and the pressure of trying to fix ourselves, fix others, or fix our circumstances—and we are frustrated because we can't. But the truth is, we were never meant to do all of this by self-effort.

Grace is for saving us, and it is also for transforming us.

As I continually made the choice to wrestle, I began to realize that as much as I sang about grace, read about grace, and nodded in agreement about how amazing grace was, I didn't really understand grace. I began to see that even when I had nothing to give, couldn't perform, and was not an acceptable version of who I thought I should be, Jesus was there, loving me still. He was giving me what I knew I didn't deserve and didn't earn. I could cry at this unconditional love even now.

> Grace is for saving us, and it is also for transforming us.

You see, I was six when I chose to follow Jesus, so my experience of saving grace was limited. Grace is something you have to experience on a very personal level in order to be thankful for it, and my wrestling began to reveal how beautiful it really was.

When we have nothing to give but broken pieces and God takes them and makes something beautiful out of them, that, my friend, is grace. We start relying on God's grace when we see that something in our lives is impossibly broken and we choose to confess that God must do for us what we cannot do for ourselves. We are not required to figure out steps ahead of time, to make things happen by self-effort, or to bring about the change we need. Our responsibility in it all is to confess, to surrender, and to wait for God to do what only He can do.

In our wrestling seasons, we see that we don't just need a Savior once at salvation, but every day thereafter as well. Today, tomorrow, and the next day—again and again. Like little children, we throw our hands upward and cry, "Save me!"

MORE THAN WE ARE NOW

Why do we dare choose this wrestle? Why grapple with the Lord as He reveals what we haven't yet realized? Because we are called to be more than we are now, and this is how we get there.

When we hang on to God in our hardest moments, we can't always see how He is working things together for our good, but the Lord promises He is doing just that (Romans 8:28). It may feel impossible, but when we continue to rely on God's grace and strength, we will see things on the other side of our struggles that we never thought possible. We accept the invitation to wrestle with God because this is how He has chosen to reveal to us the wounds we are denying and the lies we are believing.

Keep holding on, my friend. There is healing, truth, and unconditional love found at the foot of the cross. When we choose to trust Him, take up our cross, and let Him reveal to us the ways in which we have misplaced our hopes, He is faithful to lavish us with the grace we so desperately need.

4

WHEN YOU CAN NO LONGER PRETEND

All battles are first
won or lost, in the mind.

JOAN OF ARC,
fifteenth-century martyr
and patron saint of France

I WAS FOURTEEN WEEKS PREGNANT with my second child and
two years into my long and tiring wrestle. The Lord had patiently
been contending with me through my frustration and disappointment, and He was beginning to remove the toxic roots He had
exposed. I knew He was with me, but the battle was on, and I was
exhausted deep within my soul.

Sitting at the kitchen table with my laptop, I tried to muster the
energy to write a blog post, but all I could think about was how awful
I felt. I was tired, sore, suffering from heartburn, and breaking out in
body acne. I felt guilty for not being the kind of mom who cherishes
every moment of pregnancy like other moms. I wanted to be perceived as a good mom, but I could no longer pretend I felt that way.

It hit me in that moment how much pressure I was putting on

myself to perform—for God, for my family, and so that I could be okay with myself. But my attempts to perform only led to deep guilt when who I really was showed up and laughed in the face of fake Ashley.

For example, when my husband and I would go out to eat, performing Ashley wanted to be a money-conscious, responsible, and thoughtful wife. So I would order something inexpensive that I didn't really want because if I ordered something more expensive that I did want, I wouldn't be living up to the role I thought I needed to play. But real Ashley? She would show up and get mad at Daniel for ordering whatever he wanted regardless of the cost. He never once said I had to choose a less expensive option, and I never once asked him to do the same. But he didn't know the roles I thought we were all supposed to be living up to, and so he never tried to live up to them. The nerve of someone not living up to the unspoken expectations I put on myself!

Unfortunately, my experience growing up in the church only intensified the need I felt to perform. I wanted to do it all right, to be seen as right—not just to be right for its own sake, but to prove I loved God and wanted to please Him. In reality, I was performing for acceptance, for approval, and to somehow convince myself I was worthy of the love I received from God and everyone who loved Him.

My childhood teachers no doubt had good and holy intentions, but what I learned from them at a young age was a lot of "shoulds" about what to do when I was struggling: "You should have more faith," or "You should have more of a servant's heart," or "You should just trust the Lord more, and you will be fixed." But when things got really bad and I moved into a place of weakness and weariness I had never experienced before, the shoulds failed me. In fact, I wished with all my heart that what I needed to do to feel better were that easy.

I closed my laptop and gazed out the kitchen window. What I genuinely wanted was not so much to be fixed but to be loved and valued even when I couldn't perform, even when I couldn't do all the serving or come up with all the solutions. I wanted someone to see me and tell me that my life still mattered and to rescue me from this, whatever this was. But I had been trying so long and so hard to be seen and validated by others that I was exhausted. I knew what I really needed was a Savior, and I already had one.

In my wrestle with the Lord, I had once asked Him to define me, to show me who I was—and He did. My calling was to join Him in fulfilling the promises of Isaiah 61—to bind up the brokenhearted, to bring into the light those who sit in darkness, and to speak freedom to captives. Sitting at the kitchen table, I believed that was still God's call on my life, but I was also coming to realize that all those promises applied to me as well. *I* was brokenhearted, sitting in darkness, and feeling like a captive—and I needed to be bound up, to be brought into the light, to be freed. I needed a Savior.

What my Savior had been gently whispering to me at this stage of my journey was this: *Stop pretending, Ashley. Stop pretending to have it all together, to be okay when you're not. Stop getting others to tell you your worth and striving for others to recognize your value. I am the only one who can give you those things—and I want to.*

I also needed to stop trying to do things for God—to earn His acceptance, to be worthy of His love. I knew He wanted me to truly believe deep down that He loved me simply because I was His daughter, not because of what I could do for Him. I was exhausted because I had been trying for too long to be my own savior, and that was never God's intent. I had relied on self-effort to be good enough when that is exactly what Jesus had died to set me free from.

I knew the truth of all this in my head but not yet in my heart.

I wanted to need Him. I wanted to truly believe that nothing was better than Jesus—that no one else could save me, love me, or give me my identity. I wanted Him to be life to me. I wanted to know what it meant to feel His great redemption—not logically or on paper, but in my heart because I had experienced it. And maybe that was what I was finally beginning to experience now.

Stop pretending, Ashley.

I knew He was inviting me to a new and deeper place. It was an invitation to walk with Him through these hard choices I faced. Would I dare to let go of my need to perform and my need to live up to who I thought I was supposed to be? Could I recognize that I was still trying to prove to Him and to everyone else that I was worthy of His love? Could I learn what it meant to accept His love even when I felt least deserving of it? Through the hopelessness and the brokenness, I didn't understand what all of this might mean, but He did. It would mean letting go of everything else. He needed to be my only option. No matter what, He needed to be enough.

ALONE WITH GOD

As frightening as it may be to come to a place where God is our only option, it's also essential when we're tired of trying. Author and pastor Warren Wiersbe writes, "When we're alone and at the end of our resources, then God can come to us and do something in us. . . . When we're alone, we can't . . . be distracted; we have to live with ourselves and face ourselves."[1] And that's precisely where Jacob found himself: "Jacob was left alone. And a man wrestled with him until the breaking of the day" (Genesis 32:24).

Sometimes when we feel stuck in our hardships and fears, we shame ourselves for not being able to move on or "get over it." But God is not as impatient with us as we are with ourselves. We have expectations of ourselves—to be better, to know better, and to be stronger. We reason that struggles like this happen to other people, not us. We've always been the ones who helped and had wisdom and advice for others. Now, this person staring back at us in the mirror, the one who seems broken beyond recognition and has nothing to offer, feels unfamiliar and maybe even humiliating.

Was that the way Jacob felt in the moment he was left all alone? One scholar's assessment of Jacob's emotional state makes me feel like Jacob and I could have really understood each other:

> It is natural to suppose that Jacob remained behind to think and to pray at this crisis of his life. He was given over to anxious fears; the darkness and loneliness intensified them. The thought that God had left him, or was opposed to him, overwhelmed him.[2]

Do any emotions in that description sound familiar to you?
Anxious fears.
Darkness.
Loneliness.

If so, it's probably not hard for you to understand what Jacob was going through. Despite all his possessions, accomplishments, and family members, Jacob was completely alone in this moment and full of fear and dread. There were no more distractions, nothing but the naked reality of what he was facing and a God he wasn't sure would answer him.

God had called Jacob to face some things he had been running from, and now he was in a terrifying position, one he had never faced before. His past was familiar and safe—he knew how to work for his father-in-law and how to care for his family. He understood his identity and what he had to offer in those places. In fact, it's reasonable to assume he had a certain amount of pride in all he had accomplished and accumulated. We see this when he sent the messengers to Esau, saying, "I have oxen, donkeys, flocks, male servants, and female servants. I have sent to tell my lord, in order that I may find favor in your sight" (Genesis 32:5). But as Jacob stood alone on the cliff edge of an uncertain future, nothing was familiar and safe. God was asking him to face the fact that all the ways he had pretended and performed up to this point wouldn't help him, not in this.

Alone, Jacob made the hard choice to grapple with God. God needed Jacob to see that what he possessed and what he could do were not who he was. He no longer had the identity that had defined him for decades, and his possessions and accomplishments could not save him from what was to come.

Would we dare make this same hard choice to stop performing for God? It's a frightening choice to make when performing has been our go-to strategy and our means of knowing if we are good enough. As much as we want to stop performing because we are so exhausted, we also believe performing is what "good Christians do." We shame ourselves when we can't perform because we wonder, *What will they think about my love for God? If I stop performing, will the worst of who I am be unleashed?*

If you struggle with questions like these, try thinking about them relationally instead. You're probably familiar with the statement, "Christianity is about a relationship, not a religion." You may have even nodded in agreement when you heard it in a sermon or read it in a Bible study. But what intimate relationship have you ever known that is based on performance? What kind of intimacy would be possible between two people if one felt like they could never be honest, always had to have it together, and felt ashamed for never measuring up? An unhealthy one, that is for sure.

As you read the following definition of intimacy, consider if this is how you feel in your relationship with God.

Intimacy in a relationship is a feeling of being close, and emotionally connected and supported. It means being able to share a whole range of thoughts, feelings, and experiences that

Whom Did Jacob Wrestle?

The Genesis 32 passage describes Jacob's wrestling opponent this way: "Jacob was left alone. And a man wrestled with him until the breaking of the day" (Genesis 32:24). In the same passage, the man also said to Jacob, "You have struggled with God" (Genesis 32:28, NIV). Later, the prophet Hosea wrote that Jacob "wrestled with the angel and won" (Hosea 12:4, NLT). So why do we say Jacob wrestled with God?

To answer that question, it helps to understand something scholars call a *theophany*, which is "any temporary, normally visible, manifestation of God."[4] Examples of theophanies in the Bible include the burning bush (Exodus 3:2-6), the smoke and fire that descended on Mt. Sinai at the giving of the law (Exodus 19:18), the heavenly voice and dove at Jesus' baptism (Matthew 3:16), and the flames that signified the coming of the Holy Spirit (Acts 2:2). Another form of theophany is what biblical writers sometimes refer to as the "angel of the Lord," which appears more than fifty times in the Old Testament. Although the Genesis text describes Jacob's opponent as a man, Jacob named the place he wrestled *Peniel*, meaning "face of God," which shows he understood it to be a divine encounter.

we have as human beings. It involves being open and talking through your thoughts and emotions, letting your guard down (being vulnerable), and showing someone else how you feel and what your hopes and dreams are. . . . Intimacy is achieved when we become close to someone else and are reassured that we are loved and accepted for who we are.[3]

True intimacy and performance cannot coexist. To know we are truly accepted, we must choose to be vulnerable and honest, especially with God. When we choose instead to lean on our showmanship, God must challenge this in us. Not because He is mad at us, but to show us a more beautiful way. He knows that our heart behind it all has been to please Him, to love others, and to do our very best for Him. But somewhere along the way, that desire to please Him became about us instead—about our strength, about how we could make a plan, about how we could work hard enough, and about how God would be proud of all our efforts.

True intimacy and performance cannot coexist.

In the process, we lost track of the truth that we will never be able to perform enough to earn God's love and approval. That is what God wants to show us in this season as we stand face-to-face alone with Him. God desires true intimacy with you and me. He doesn't want our trying hard; He wants our hearts. He needs us to know that, like any good father, He loves us because we are His and not because we can do a lot for Him. And even when we can't do a thing, He is still just as in love with us. This is safety; this is true love. It comes with no conditions. And to help us discover this, God meets us alone and engages us in this wrestle as we make the hard choice to continue the fight.

GOD CHOOSES THE HONEST
NOT THE PERFECT

Intimacy requires vulnerability, and vulnerability requires letting ourselves be seen and loved as we are and not as we wish we were. In our comparison-saturated world, we are tempted multiple times a day to believe that unpolished, unfiltered, regular old us is far from enough. But God loves (and I do mean *loves*) to use the most unlikely people to do extraordinary things. When God shows up and does the impossible with those who are honest about all they lack, no one is more surprised than the people themselves.

> **G**od loves (and I do mean *loves*) to use the most unlikely people to do extraordinary things.

If we could sit down with Jacob, maybe he would tell us he was scared to be honest with God. He knew he had made some major mistakes and that his life had become something of a disaster. How could God still love him, or why would God still choose him to pass on a blessing he had stolen? Jacob had been running from his past and relying on his own abilities to get him through for his whole life. He wanted to be who God had created him to be, and he was trying his absolute best to be that. If he was trying hard, then why was every try a fail? Maybe because God didn't want Jacob to try, He wanted him to surrender. And the only way to surrender was to be honest.

We see this with so many people God chose to use throughout Scripture. They were flawed, ordinary folks who were honest about who they were. God chose, loved, and used these people despite their flaws because they were willing to depend on Him. God isn't looking for a show but for us to show up. As He did for these heroes in the Bible, He wants to meet us in the middle of our fears and our struggles. He invites us to be honest about our lack and to make the hard choice to move forward—not because of who we are and all we can do, but because of who He is. No pretending needed.

Let's look at some examples of people God invited to be honest about their lack and how He used them in powerful ways.

Gideon

Gideon lived in a time when God's people had fallen into idolatry by worshiping Baal. As a consequence, God left them at the mercy of the Midianites, their enemy, for seven years. When the Israelites cried out to God for help, God chose an unlikely man named Gideon to be their deliverer. God met him on an ordinary day when he was doing ordinary things.

> Gideon was beating out wheat in the winepress to hide it from the Midianites. And the angel of the LORD appeared to him and said to him, "The LORD is with you, O mighty man of valor." And Gideon said to him, "Please, my lord, if the LORD is with us, why then has all this happened to us? And where are all his wonderful deeds that our fathers recounted to us, saying, 'Did not the LORD bring us up from Egypt?' But now the LORD has forsaken us and given us into the hand of Midian." And the LORD turned to him and said, "Go in this might of yours and save Israel from the hand of Midian; do not I send you?" And he said to him, "Please, Lord, how can I save Israel? Behold, my clan is the weakest in Manasseh, and I am the least in my father's house." And the LORD said to him, "But I will be with you, and you shall strike the Midianites as one man."
> **JUDGES 6:11-16**

Gideon was doing his chores and trying to hide the crops from Israel's enemies when the Lord appeared to him. Gideon confessed, "Not me! I am the weakest!" And it's as if God said, "Great! My favorite kind!" In response to his honest confession of weakness, God told Gideon who he could be because of the Lord's power—a "mighty man of valor."

Gideon had questions and he pushed back, just as we sometimes do when our circumstances seem at odds with what we consider evidence of God's presence. With Gideon, we wonder, *If God is with me, why have all these bad things happened to me?* Perhaps Gideon, too, was tired of trying. It seems clear he felt abandoned by God in the midst of Israel's hardships, but that was not where the story ended. It only seemed that way from Gideon's limited perspective.

Notice how the Lord affirmed Gideon's identity when He said, "Go in this might of *yours* and save Israel from the hand of Midian." And then God added, "Do not I send you?" (Judges 6:14, emphasis added). In other words, "Even if your own might weren't enough, you have all of my might behind you!" This was Gideon's hard choice. Would he allow his weakness and all he had seen up until now to define him? Or would he allow God to define him?

God never does anything without a reason. There is a reason God allowed this interaction to occur and a reason He allowed Gideon to ask for proof—which He later gave to help Gideon continue to trust Him. God patiently allowed Gideon to process what was happening to him so Gideon would trust that this was God's plan. And just as God said he would, Gideon went on to conquer the Midianites in extraordinary ways.

Gideon's weakness didn't disqualify him from what God wanted to do in and through him. It was in response to his honest confession that God then spoke Gideon's true identity and his purpose—to be a "mighty man of valor" who would conquer Israel's enemies.

The Widow of Zarephath

The story of Elijah and the widow of Zarephath is another great example of God choosing someone who was honest about their lack. Elijah had prophesied a drought would come because the evil King Ahab and Queen Jezebel had greatly dishonored the Lord. The Lord then told Elijah to go hide by a brook and ravens would come and feed him. But when the brook dried up, the Lord directed Elijah to a widow in Zarephath who would feed him. When Elijah found the woman and asked her for bread, she responded,

> "As surely as the LORD your God lives," she replied, "I don't have any bread—only a handful of flour in a jar and a little olive oil in a jug. I am gathering a few sticks to take home and make a meal for myself and my son, that we may eat it—and die."
>
> Elijah said to her, "Don't be afraid. Go home and do as you have said. But first make a small loaf of bread for me from what you have and bring it to me, and then make something for yourself and your son. For this is what the LORD, the God of Israel, says: 'The jar of flour will not be used up and the jug of oil will not run dry until the day the LORD sends rain on the land.'"
> 1 KINGS 17:12-14, NIV

The widow of Zarephath was the very definition of being tired of trying. In fact, there was nothing left to try, and she was resigned to the fact that she and her son would soon die. All she could see was that they were out of food, and this had to be the end.

When Elijah approached her, she immediately recognized he was a man of God, and it would have been the custom to provide what she could for him. But immediately, in her desperation for herself and her son, she confessed the reality in which they found themselves. They did not have enough to even go on living themselves.

Why did God send Elijah, who was in need, to a woman who didn't have what either of them needed to survive? Perhaps this was a test of faith. As she walked in those desperate moments in need of provision, God required something from her, even in her own perceived lack. When Elijah asked her to bake him bread after she had already confessed her lack, the woman had to risk the little she had to feed Elijah first. They were both vulnerably exposed, and yet God asked them to move ahead in faith anyway.

This was the widow's hard choice. Would she trust God and put what little she had left on the line of faith? Or would she trust her own lack?

Elijah encouraged the woman. He told her not to be afraid, to go home and do as she planned, but to first make a small meal for him. He spoke the promises and provisions of God to her and invited her to take these steps of faith even though they likely made no sense to her.

Acting in faith, the widow gave her tiny portion, her very last lifeline, to God's prophet. And just as Elijah had said, God provided more than enough to feed the widow and her son. The lesson she learned that day was that her lack did not define who she was. God didn't ask the widow for what she didn't have. He asked her to trust Him with what she did.

Elijah

It wasn't long before Elijah, the prophet who had seen God provide time and time again—the same Elijah who had just experienced

God's provision through the widow at Zarephath—found himself
doubting again. While he had faith when the widow was in need, he
still struggled when he reached the point of being tired of trying in
his own life. He had been charged with a scary and difficult task, to
confront King Ahab and Queen Jezebel about their idolatry and to
show the people of Israel that Baal was not the true God.

After a showdown in which God revealed Himself to be the true
God and Baal, their idol, was exposed as a fraud, Queen Jezebel was
furious and vowed to kill Elijah.

> Elijah was afraid and ran for his life. When he came to
> Beersheba in Judah, he left his servant there, while he himself
> went a day's journey into the wilderness. He came to a broom
> bush, sat down under it and prayed that he might die. "I have
> had enough, LORD," he said. "Take my life; I am no better than
> my ancestors." Then he lay down under the bush and fell
> asleep.
>
> All at once an angel touched him and said, "Get up and
> eat." He looked around, and there by his head was some bread
> baked over hot coals, and a jar of water. He ate and drank and
> then lay down again.
>
> The angel of the LORD came back a second time and
> touched him and said, "Get up and eat, for the journey is too
> much for you." So he got up and ate and drank.
>
> Strengthened by that food, he traveled forty days and forty
> nights until he reached Horeb, the mountain of God.
> 1 KINGS 19:3-8, NIV

Elijah was exhausted and despairing. And it's interesting to note
that he reached this point not after disobedience or failure but after

walking closely with God and performing an incredible miracle in God's power. In fact, it was his ministry success that led Jezebel to vow to kill him. Despite all he had experienced of God's provision and power, Elijah was terrified and felt like he could no longer go on—to the point that he asked God to take his life.

Even in this, God responded to Elijah's honesty about his desperation. When Elijah said he didn't have anything left in him to perform or give, God's first response was to send an angel to minister to Elijah's physical needs. The angel touched him and said, "Get up and eat." And then the angel of the Lord returned and encouraged and cared for Elijah again, saying, "Get up and eat, for the journey is too much for you."

The Lord knew Elijah was exhausted, and before asking Elijah to move on, God provided rest and nourishment. It mattered to God that Elijah was strengthened. God provided for Elijah's needs because God doesn't just love what we do for Him, He loves *us*—and He understands our very real human needs and limitations. God was not indifferent toward Elijah's suffering and discouragement, and He is not indifferent to your suffering or mine.

After resting and eating, Elijah knew there was still more ahead. More to be said, more to be seen, more to be done. Would Elijah trust God and continue the journey, or would he resign himself to exhaustion and despair, refusing to acknowledge the ways God was providing?

This was Elijah's hard choice. Would he choose, yet again, to move forward in faith? Or would he give up and resign himself to despair?

Let's read on just a little further, because the beauty of a relationship with the Lord when we are in some of the hardest times of our lives is on full display here.

And the word of the LORD came to him: "What are you doing here, Elijah?"

He replied, "I have been very zealous for the LORD God Almighty. The Israelites have rejected your covenant, torn down your altars, and put your prophets to death with the sword. I am the only one left, and now they are trying to kill me too."

The LORD said, "Go out and stand on the mountain in the presence of the LORD, for the LORD is about to pass by."

Then a great and powerful wind tore the mountains apart and shattered the rocks before the LORD, but the LORD was not in the wind. After the wind there was an earthquake, but the LORD was not in the earthquake. After the earthquake came a fire, but the LORD was not in the fire. And after the fire came a gentle whisper. When Elijah heard it, he pulled his cloak over his face and went out and stood at the mouth of the cave.

1 KINGS 19:9-13, NIV

God began with a question, "What are you doing here, Elijah?"(1 Kings 19:9). But God wasn't asking for information or because He was unclear about how Elijah had ended up there. He asked to give Elijah a chance to say what was true—that he had moved away from where God had told him to be. And Elijah was honest in voicing his fear and disappointment—that his ministry had failed and his life was at risk despite how faithful he had been. Now, he felt alone and so very afraid.

Something I find interesting in the Bible is how God rarely responds directly to complaints by explaining things. Instead, the Lord goes straight to the truth, straight to the heart. With Elijah, it was no different. When Elijah lamented his situation, God didn't explain the reasons why everything happened the way it did. Instead,

He revealed Himself to Elijah. God simply told Elijah to go stand out-side and wait. Elijah did this and watched as a powerful wind passed, then an earthquake and a fire, and finally a whisper from the Lord. I love commentator Matthew Henry's observation about this moment:

> The wind, and earthquake, and fire, did not make him cover his face, but the still voice did. Gracious souls are more affected by the tender mercies of the Lord, than by his terrors. The mild voice of Him who speaks from the cross, or the mercy-seat, is accompanied with peculiar power in taking possession of the heart.[5]

In that moment, Elijah didn't need a great show of power and might to restore his trust in God. What he needed was to know that God was still with him. Elijah had nothing to offer in those moments; he was tired and empty, but God met him where he was, cared for him, and spoke to him.

In all three of these examples—Gideon, the widow, and Elijah—God wasn't looking for individuals who had enough, who weren't weak, or who considered themselves capable of doing what He asked of them. On the contrary, God chose to use people who were honest with Him about their lack. They did not and could not pretend like they had more than they did, which was basically nothing. So, if we feel like we have very little today, why not be honest with God about that and make the hard choice to trust that He is the God who makes something miraculous and powerful out of our nothing?

GOD STILL LOVES YOU

Maybe we have seen God move mountains, break chains, or do mir-acles in our lives and in the lives of others in the past, and we wonder why He is not doing these things anymore. We don't have to be afraid of our questions and doubts because God sees our needs and invites us to bring them into His presence. While we would love to see these big acts of God, the ones He is more than capable of doing, what our hearts really need to know is that when we are empty, when we're tired, when we can't stop the tears from falling and have nothing left to give, even then He is not waiting for us to get it together but is with us and loving us in our suffering.

When we show up to serve God, to offer what we have, to go and do and be all He is asking of us, we sometimes think He loves us only for what we have to offer. We have relied on what we believe we bring to the relationship, or at least on our ability to keep trying. But when we see these and many other characters in the Bible who found themselves in the exact same place, we get a picture of how God truly sees us. God is not distant or disapproving of our questions, our disappointments, or even our defeats. Instead, He invites us to speak what is on our hearts and then to move forward—not in our own strength but in His. When we make the decision to wrestle with God, we begin to move from performing for God to intimacy with Him.

It is incredibly hard to love and trust a God whom we honestly believe is disappointed in us or who withholds His love from us when we can't perform correctly for Him. But today, God wants you to know:

When you're tired . . . I still love you.
When you're devastated . . . I still love you.
When you're always sad and can't figure out why . . . I still love you.
When you have nothing left . . . I still love you.
When you are full of doubt . . . I still love you.
When your heart is broken . . . I still love you.
When you feel rejected . . . I still love you.

When you have nothing to give back . . . I still love you.
When you fail . . . I still love you.

Allow me to whisper something to your weary heart today: *God is not more in love with a future, holier version of you.* He loves you now, fully. Not only that, He is calling you into this wrestle to set you free. He wants you to believe He loves you even in your brokenness and mess.

> **God is not more in love with a future, holier version of you.**

God is not in a rush. He does not shame you for being where you are. He is with you in your dark night as you make these hard choices. He is waiting to speak the truth to you, to care for you, to ask you to keep trusting Him no matter how little you feel you have to offer right now.

We must move away from the lie that God is mad at us for not measuring up. He isn't. He knows we can't measure up, and that is why He sent Jesus. While we may know this intellectually and say we believe it, when we reach the point of being tired of trying, we still fall back on the lie that we have lost His love and approval—and that is not true.

Yes, God calls us to obedience and there is always more for us to learn, accomplish, and grow through, but without the heart knowledge of the strong and steady foundation of His love, we will continue to live insecure and untrusting.

This is going to take some work and some time. If you have always found your worth in what you can do and how well you can do it, it might feel counterintuitive to allow God to love you simply because you are His child. But remember this: God knew exactly who He was getting when He chose you. He knew your strengths and gifts, and He also knew your weaknesses and the seasons when you would get weary or weak—and He chose you still.

If you have your phone nearby, pick it up and look at how much battery life is left. If you use it long enough, you know the battery will get low and eventually die. But you'd be crazy to throw away your phone simply because the battery needs to be recharged. You don't throw out your phone because you know the problem is not the phone but the fact that it's gone too long without being plugged into its power source. The amount of battery charge does not change how valuable the phone is even when, in its uncharged condition, it can't function as intended.

Every time you plug in your phone, ask yourself if you need to be plugged into your Source as well. God meets you in the wrestle to reveal how much you need Him and to give you what your weak and weary soul requires. When you are filled up with Him, you can go longer, do what is required of you, and function as you are intended to.

Your value is unchangeable, regardless of how you feel. God is not asking you to give what you don't have, nor does He expect you to pretend you're okay when you're not. Instead, He is asking you to let go of the need you might feel to play a role and just give yourself to Him in your weakness, tiredness, and all. When you make that hard choice, you can find true intimacy with Him and trust His heart for you.

PART 2

STRUGGLING WITH GOD

PRACTICING SURRENDER

I've grown most not from victories,
but setbacks. If winning is God's reward,
then losing is how he teaches us.

SERENA WILLIAMS,
professional tennis player,
entrepreneur, and philanthropist

AFTER FEEDING THE KIDS BREAKFAST, I walked to the sliding glass door at the back of our apartment to watch the snow falling across the parking lot. I had often joked about being Rapunzel when we lived in that apartment because the building sat high on a hill, and our unit was at the very top of the complex. And maybe it wasn't just because the building was built like a tower, but because I also felt trapped. Anxiety still filled my lungs as I took a deep breath and let out my familiar sigh, but I also felt a small stirring of hope. I was daring to believe that today would be different. It was January 1, and that meant new beginnings and leaving the old behind.

Things had been so hard, but I felt I was finally ready for more of what God had for me. Life had been far from perfect, but it seemed to have eased up a bit. I was also determined that this was the year

I was going to get in shape, though I sighed at the thought of that too. If I were honest, it had been the year to get in shape and lose weight every year because I never really got around to doing it. But I brushed off my doubts and embraced my determination. Knowing we had no plans for the day, I decided to start the New Year off right with a workout.

I wandered to the bedroom and considered going for a walk but realized it would be too hard to walk through the snow or I might slip, and so I decided against it. Instead, without bothering to change out of what were probably my oldest pajama pants, complete with holes, I tied up my unwashed hair and put on an old workout video. This was going to be a new and better year.

Like every year, I had written out my goals and had chosen one word to focus on for the year. This year it was *listen*, and I was guardedly excited to see what focusing on that word might reveal to me in the months ahead.

As I pushed the workout DVD into the player, I began to think about how things had slowly started changing as I entered into this season of letting the Lord uncover issues that He wanted to wrestle through with me. I was determined to take action and do everything within my power to discover the lessons, to learn them, and then to move on—as quickly as possible. I just wanted to be out of this thing. To that end, I had spent a lot of time searching for a counselor. I hadn't pursued counseling previously because we simply couldn't afford it. I knew God was helping me when I found a student who was doing a counseling internship and offered her services at no charge. It was exactly what I needed, and I went weekly for three months. I was taking every positive step forward I could, and I was starting to feel somewhat normal again—one small choice at a time.

Standing in my messy bedroom, I pressed play on the DVD and

began working out, feeling so proud of myself for starting off on the right foot. However, when I stepped backward into a lunge, my foot landed on my son's baby blanket, and I slipped. I fell to the floor and was immediately in excruciating pain. When I looked down at my leg, I saw that my kneecap was dislocated, stuck on the outside of my leg. I screamed in pain.

Daniel ran into the room, his eyes wide in panic. We both knew I needed help, but we lived in Rapunzel's tower at the top of this apartment complex and there was no way he could get me out of there on his own.

"Call 911!" I yelled.

"No! What?" Daniel responded in disbelief. Even with my screaming, it hadn't really hit him how serious this was. But I knew this was bad—really bad.

Daniel made the call, and the paramedics came a few moments later. I heard their sirens echoing across the parking lot I had been gazing at minutes before, and soon there were five of them standing over me. I was deeply regretting this workout, not to mention the fact that I was wearing the least presentable pajamas I owned.

It was humiliating as well as painful.

I screamed every time the paramedics touched me. I had envisioned them shooting me up with some meds and popping my knee back into place right then and there, but that was not what happened. Instead, they brought in a strange-looking chair and explained that they were about to carry me out on it and down to the ambulance. When they asked my weight before picking me up, I felt even more humiliated. Then they proceeded to strap my leg into a brace as best they could, lift me into the chair contraption, and carry me down the fifty-two steps between our apartment and the ambulance. Believe me, I counted them later.

Excruciating does not begin to describe the descent. Every tiny motion made me feel like my leg was about to rip open.

Even in my crisis state of mind, I couldn't help but ask the Lord, "Why?" We were struggling financially, and I felt hopeless knowing how much the ambulance would cost, not to mention the hospital. The old critical voices rushed over me, *You are such a burden, Ashley! And you thought things were getting better? Ha!* The faint glimmer of hope I'd had that things were improving was now mocking me.

As the paramedics carried me down, I alternately cried out in pain and then apologized to them and any neighbors who had come out to see what on earth was happening in their stairwell.

They loaded me into the back of the ambulance, my first ride ever, and I watched Daniel quickly load the kids into the car to follow behind. As soon as we got to the hospital, the doctors put me under, reset my knee, and sent me home with crutches and instructions to call an orthopedic doctor.

What a start to a new year. I wanted to crumble. After everything we had been dealing with, now this? What was I going to do? Daniel worked ridiculously long hours, and I had a four-year-old and a four-month-old to care for.

The next day, I hobbled my way around on crutches with my leg in a brace. I precariously pushed my baby from place to place on a rolling office chair until my parents arrived to help me for the day. I still couldn't believe that all this had happened on what I thought— what I hoped—was the beginning of a new and better season.

After my parents left that evening and Daniel had returned home, I was finally in bed relaxing and decided to write a prayer about how helpless and hopeless I felt: *Dear Lord, I do not understand what is happening, and I am afraid. I can no longer handle this; I feel like I am drowning! Please be for me what I need, do for our family what only you can do. All that I have to give you is a broken heart that does not know where to go from here. You say you are my strength; please be that for me today. In Jesus' name, amen.*

I closed my journal and rolled over to get myself out of bed when I suddenly felt a "pop."

A surge of horror rose from the bottom of my gut and out of my mouth, "No, no, no, no!"

My knee was out of its socket *again*.

I immediately cried out to the Lord for a miracle. *Please, Lord, not again. Please put my kneecap back in place. I can't do this again. I can't go through this one more time. We can't afford this. Why, Lord. Why?*

Daniel ran into the room and looked as shocked and horrified as I was at what he saw. We both felt paralyzed, and we were waiting, hoping, crying out to the Lord to put my kneecap back where it belonged. But when no miracle intervention materialized, we went through the whole process again.

We initially called my parents, hoping that they could help. They agreed to drive over to the house but instructed us to call emergency services again. As the paramedics wheeled me past my dad, who had been a firefighter for thirty years, I knew he could do nothing for me. In that moment, I had such a painful thought. *My actual, earthly dad is here, and he can do nothing for me, but I know he would if he could. So, why, Lord? I know you love me. Why aren't you doing something when you can? Why is this happening to me again?*

As the paramedics once again put me into the back of the ambulance, a strange peace came over me. It was a hands-up-in-surrender moment because I knew everything was so completely out of my control.

My word this year is listen, *Lord. Well, I'm listening. What, Lord? What? I cannot do this anymore. I do not understand. I give up.*

In my spirit, I felt Him ask, "Will you trust me, even when I say no again?"

A knowing came over me. I was going to have to walk through this hard season I didn't understand and didn't want—and I had a choice to make. Would I choose to walk through it with Him or without Him?

It was another invitation to wrestle—to let go of the outcomes and embrace the process in this struggle with God.

UNKNOWN STRENGTH

When we last checked in with Jacob, he was afraid, anxious, and alone when God engaged him in a wrestle that lasted all night long. Here's what happened next: "When the man saw that he did not prevail against Jacob, he touched his hip socket, and Jacob's hip was put out of joint as he wrestled with him" (Genesis 32:25).

This verse is a bit shocking. What could it possibly mean that Jacob's opponent could not prevail against him? Surely God could overpower one human being, right? Many Bible commentators agree that perhaps God purposely held back, waiting for Jacob to recognize his own need to surrender. Whatever the case, Jacob was being enabled, even in this struggle with God, to embrace the process no matter how difficult and long it might be.

Jacob had prayed, "Please deliver me from the hand of my brother, from the hand of Esau, for I fear him, that he may come and attack me, the mothers with the children" (Genesis 32:11). Jacob's request was for deliverance, but God's answer was a wrestle.

God could just as easily have sent a messenger telling Jacob not to fear, that everything would work out better than he expected it to, but He didn't. Instead, He met Jacob Himself to confront what needed to be confronted. This wrestle was about more than just the pain, the confusion, and the exhaustion. It was about more than the unknowns of Jacob's impending confrontation with his brother. This was about what was happening inside of Jacob, something God could no longer allow to go unaddressed. This was about Jacob's beliefs about himself and about God. It was about what God was calling Jacob to believe and the purpose God wanted him to walk in.

Jacob needed to realize that it was God's strength and wisdom, not his own, that he needed. Until Jacob recognized that what he had was insufficient, God could not give him what he really needed. *The wrestle exposes our self-reliance and reveals our need for surrender.*

Remember, Jacob was a regular human being who, at this moment, was no doubt in excruciating pain because of something the Lord Himself had done to him. Jacob was locked in a wrestle, desperate for answers to his prayers, and yet the one whom he hoped would rescue him had wounded him instead. This was both terrible and unbearable.

When a hip is put out of the socket it causes severe pain, and it's impossible to bear weight on that leg. The fight was over, and Jacob was left in excruciating physical pain. He could no longer stand and there was no fight left in him. Trying hard in his own strength was over.

Like Jacob, we experience times in our lives when our disappointments, fears, or hardships begin to reveal all the places where we have relied not on God but on our own strength, ability, and reasoning to save us. Even if we have been declaring all the while that we need and want to rely on God, it isn't until we are confronted with our own utter weakness that we begin to understand we have been quite happy to get by on our own strength and abilities.

In the sport of wrestling, there is a hold called a "submission." It is defined this way: "In combat sports a submission hold (colloquially referred to as a 'submission') is a grappling hold that is applied with the purpose of forcing an opponent to submit out of either extreme pain or fear of injury."[1] That's a pretty good description of the move God makes when we refuse to surrender to Him out of sheer stubbornness. As author and pastor Tony Evans says, "God will put you in a bad situation not because He's trying to hurt you but because He is trying to change you."[2] When nothing else works, it's often the pain of our situation that finally breaks this streak of stubbornness that insists we are fine on our own and that we don't need God.

This lesson about surrender isn't unique to Jacob; it's one that everyone who follows Christ has to learn sooner or later. Here's how the apostle Paul describes his own wrestle and surrender:

> So to keep me from becoming conceited because of the surpassing greatness of the revelations, a thorn was given me in the flesh, a messenger of Satan to harass me, to keep me from becoming conceited. Three times I pleaded with the Lord about this, that it should leave me. But he said to me, "My grace is sufficient for you, for my power is made perfect in weakness." Therefore, I will boast all the more gladly of my weaknesses, so that the power of Christ may rest upon me.
>
> 2 CORINTHIANS 12:7-9

If we have grown up in or around the church, we may be very familiar with this passage, especially the part that tells us Christ's power is made perfect in weakness. But it's fascinating that Paul attributes his thorn to Satan, and twice states it was given to keep him from being conceited.

Paul, an amazing man of God who had been jailed and beaten and had given his entire life for the sake of Christ and the gospel, was given a torment to keep him from becoming conceited. What does it mean to be conceited? It means "having or showing an excessively high opinion of oneself."[3] And if we're honest, we need these moments in our lives too, because it is far too easy to be impressed with the gifts and strengths and words God has given us, rather than with God Himself. It's easy, in our humanity, to begin to lean into our own resources rather than the Source.

So what's the opposite of conceit? Humility. However, we cannot walk in humility and become more like Christ without confronting all the ways we knowingly or unknowingly rely on ourselves. *God must move us from self-reliance to God-reliance.*

Whether our struggle takes the form of thorns, wrestling, or any other experience of hardship, we can trust that God is being faithful to us within it. He knows how limited our strength is, He knows our resources and skills won't be enough, and He would not be a loving Father if He left us to our own devices. The only reason God allows any of these things to happen is to relieve us of having to be enough so we can rest securely in the promise that He is more than enough.

Hear this, friend. If you are in the middle of what feels like the hardest wrestle of your life, it is not a punishment from God. It is not a punishment at all. Let that truth settle deep into your soul. I know it can be tempting to believe that everything you're going through could have been avoided if, at some point, you had made a different choice. Maybe you have believed that God has brought judgment on you because of past mistakes, and now you have two weights to carry—one of the pain you are walking through and the other of false guilt. Be brave enough to release that to Him today. Do not carry it with you one more moment.

Even when God took the Israelites into the wilderness, it wasn't to punish them but to humble and test them. They were in the desert to begin with because He had set them free from bondage in Egypt. He had heard their cries for rescue and had delivered them from slavery. But being free physically wasn't enough. God also wanted them to be free emotionally and spiritually. In their captivity, they had learned to depend on only themselves for what they needed. Their hearts had become numb because of centuries of brutal mistreatment and deprivation. God brought them out by way of wandering because they had to recognize that their self-reliance was not enough. God wanted His people to depend on Him alone. That was the lesson woven throughout forty years of wilderness wandering, and it is the same lesson we must learn and relearn every time we make the choice to wrestle with God.

Just as Jacob had, up to this point, relied on his own strategizing and resources to get what he wanted, we tend to rely on what we can control to get what we think we need most. Perhaps, as we sometimes do, Jacob believed the promises God had spoken over his life, but instead of trusting and waiting on God, Jacob took matters into his own hands. He relied on manipulation and striving to get what he wanted when he wanted it. He became a liar and a thief in the process, and it was this identity he had come to rely on to get what he needed. But God could no longer allow self-reliance to continue in Jacob's life—and He can no longer allow it to continue in ours.

> God could no longer allow self-reliance to continue in Jacob's life—and he can no longer allow it to continue in ours.

This, my friend, is when we learn to practice surrender.

THE PRACTICE OF SURRENDER

According to *Merriam-Webster's Dictionary*, to surrender is "to yield to the power, control, or possession of another upon compulsion or demand" or "to give (oneself) up into the power of another."[4] It is no wonder most of us avoid having anything to do with surrender. Why would we willingly give ourselves into the power of another person?

However, things are a little different when it comes to surrendering to the Lord. We know that when we surrender to His control, the outcome is always for our good. Even so, sometimes it's way easier to sing about surrender in worship songs than it is to practice surrender in our everyday lives. So what does it mean to surrender to the Lord, and how do we do it? Although there are any number of ways God might invite us to surrender, here are five steps we can take to practice surrender at any time:

- Acknowledge the areas in our lives that we are struggling to control in our own power.
- Confess our fears about these areas.
- Admit we can no longer do anything without the Lord's help.
- Release our demand for specific outcomes.
- Receive God's help and strength.

To practice surrender is to acknowledge that we are tired of trying because we were never meant to try so hard in our own strength. God has brought us to this place to show us that He never expected us to figure things out on our own or have what it takes to get through our struggles without Him.

Here's a prayer you can use as a starting point:

Lord, I recognize I am trying to control _____ because I am afraid _____. I admit I have tried to overcome this on my own, and I am now fully aware of my weakness. I am asking you, Lord, to please fill me with your strength. I let go of the expectation that the outcomes must be _____ or turn out like _____. I have nothing, Lord, but you have everything I need. I am believing by faith that you are even now providing me with your strength and help.

In Jesus' name, amen.

Surrender is when things begin to change. Even when your circumstances remain the same and your questions remain unanswered, practicing surrender changes your heart and mind. It's called the "practice" of surrender because it isn't something that happens just once. In fact, it is a daily act of letting go again and again, acknowledging our powerlessness from one moment to the next, and letting God be God in our lives.

And surrender isn't the end. It is, in fact, just the beginning of all God wants to do in you and me. Jesus came to rescue us, to be our Savior; and sometimes that includes rescuing us from ourselves. We need to be saved from the belief that we have to figure it all out and get ourselves through this in our own strength. He knows we can't. But we cannot be rescued if we refuse to recognize or acknowledge our own self-reliance and our determination to get what we think we need most.

Desperation isn't a popular or desirable place to be, and most of us do our best to avoid it at all costs. But when we are desperate for the strength of our powerful God, we finally have access to the never-ending source of strength we need.

Here's how Jesus taught this principle to His disciples:

> I am the vine; you are the branches. If you remain in me and I in you, you will bear much fruit; apart from me you can do nothing. If you do not remain in me, you are like a branch that is thrown away and withers; such branches are picked up, thrown into the fire and burned. If you remain in me and my words remain in you, ask whatever you wish, and it will be done for you. This is to my Father's glory, that you bear much fruit, showing yourselves to be my disciples.
>
> **JOHN 15:5-8,** NIV

What fruit might we be missing in our lives because we are trying to produce it in our own strength? What amazing things might God have for us if we were willing to surrender, stay connected to Him, and begin to ask for His help? He has much fruit for us to bear for the Father's glory if we will only exchange reliance on our strength for His.

Will surrender always be easy? No.

Will it cost you something? Yes.

Will it be worth it? Absolutely.

When I returned from the hospital after my knee dislocated the second time, I realized I needed a way to hold on and to let go at the same time. I needed to hold on to the Lord and to the hope of what He had yet to do, but to let go of how I wanted it all to play out. My wrestle wasn't over simply because I saw my need to surrender yet again. My days were still filled with tears, frustration, and prayers that sounded like: "This hurts. I'm tired. Please help." "Please help me to trust you." "Even though this is hard, you have always been so good to me."

Holding on to God and letting go of outcomes is an essential part of every wrestle. Each prayer, each tear, each decision to hold on by faith when we just want to give up is a precious offering to the Lord.

> **Holding on to God and letting go of outcomes is an essential part of every wrestle.**

The promise of Scripture is that God has not forgotten us. The psalmist affirms God's attention and tenderness when we are struggling.

> You keep track of all my sorrows.
>> You have collected all my tears in your
>>> bottle.
>> You have recorded each one in your book.
>
> PSALM 56:8, NLT

God is not indifferent to our tears. He sees and remembers each one.

When we are struggling, we must choose to enter into the pain with God rather than trying to manage it on our own terms by running away, shutting down, getting angry, or denying the reality of what we're facing. And those options will always be a temptation when we are just so very tired of trying.

Friend, there's no doubt that surrender can be scary, and the moment we start taking a step toward it, our minds will begin to doubt and spiral with fears, especially about the ways we have been disappointed in the past. When that happens, we can be proactive by practicing truth. We can write down declarations of biblical truth and then pull them out and say them aloud to remind us of what is true.

THE PRACTICE OF TRUTH

It may feel weird at first, but speaking biblical truth out loud when we experience doubt and disappointment is an essential practice during any wrestle. The apostle Paul wrote, "So faith comes from hearing, and hearing through the word of Christ" (Romans 10:17). We must routinely speak God's words to ourselves so that truth begins to replace the lies of the old tapes that run on repeat in our minds. Perhaps you can relate to some of these lies:

- I can't believe God let this happen. God must not love me.
- Why is my life such a mess? This could never turn out well.
- I will never have enough strength to do this. I am too tired of trying.

To practice truth, we craft statements based on God's Word. That's how we speak truth over our lives. Here are some examples:

- *God deeply loves me, even when He says no.* "Humble yourselves, therefore, under the mighty hand of God so that at the proper time he may exalt you, casting all your anxieties on him, because he cares for you" (1 Peter 5:6-7).
- *My story is not over. God is not finished, and He will bring beauty from ashes.* "And I am sure of this, that he who began a good work in you will bring it to completion at the day of Jesus Christ" (Philippians 1:6).
- *Even in what I am facing, I am still blessed. I don't have to be strong because God will be my strength.* "The LORD is my strength and my defense; he has become my salvation. He is my God, and I will praise him, my father's God, and I will exalt him" (Exodus 15:2, NIV).

This is exactly what I did when God began to ask me to surrender and to change my inner dialogue to confront my thoughts of disappointment with Him. Whenever I started to have mean, discouraging thoughts or lies that I didn't want to have in my head, I began saying out loud, "I love you."

The lie I believed: "You are a burden."
The truth I replaced it with: "The LORD your God is in your midst, a mighty one who will save; he will rejoice over you with gladness; *he will quiet you by his love*; he will exult over you with loud singing" (Zephaniah 3:17, emphasis added).
"I love you, Ash."

The lie I believed: "God must be punishing me."
The truth I replaced it with: "There is no fear in *love*, but perfect

love casts out fear. For fear has to do with punishment, and whoever fears has not been perfected in love" (1 John 4:18, emphasis added).

"I love you, Ash."

Saying these truths out loud was a thought pattern interrupter. I was telling my brain, "Don't think that," by putting up a roadblock that kept my thoughts from continuing down that dark path. And I felt like every time I said, "I love you, Ash," out loud, it was God's reminder that He loved me, He was fighting for me, and together we were going to get through this.

What we think leads to actions, actions lead to patterns, and patterns dictate our lives; so this is not something we can take lightly.

I still say, "I love you, Ash," to this day, and when my family hears me say it when I am off in a corner by myself, they always respond, "Love you too." It might be a little odd, but it works.

Try saying, "I love you," or choose your own word or phrase when you need a thought pattern interrupter. The point is to be proactive about replacing misguided thoughts with simple but powerful truths.

What we think leads to actions, actions lead to patterns, and patterns dictate our lives; so this is not something we can take lightly. This is an action step we can take as we learn to surrender—to hold on to God but let go of outcomes.

ENDURING THE PAIN

Happy [is] he who learns to bear
what he cannot change.
FRIEDRICH SCHILLER,
eighteenth-century playwright,
poet, and philosopher

AFTER A FEW MONTHS OF painful physical therapy, my knee was healing, and I realized that God was doing a painful internal healing in me as well. I have found in my life that in seasons of deep healing, I cry almost uncontrollably, especially at church. This has resulted in many embarrassing moments as I bawled during worship, crying out to be saved by my Savior. There's nothing quite like having black mascara running down your cheeks only to hear the dreaded words, "Now, turn and greet your neighbor." Awkward. Apologies to every stranger's hand I shook in those moments. God and I were wrestling.

As the healing process continued, it felt as if God was continually asking me to both hold on and to let go—to hold on to Him and to let go of how I wanted it to look and when I wanted it to happen. During these days, weeks, and months, I processed a lot of grief. Grief over losing what I had always known, grief for the way I thought God was "supposed to" work in my life, grief that I was still in the middle of this after what felt like way too long. Would I make the hard choice to endure for the blessing?

Several months after my knee injury, my sister-in-law asked if I wanted to join her and my mom to train for a marathon. The thought alone felt laughable. Could my weakened and wounded knee handle such intense training? Did I even want to try? And yet, I felt the desire rise up in me and the word *audacity* rang in my ears. Would I have the audacity to attempt something so ridiculous at this time in my life?

In my heart and spirit, I believed the Lord was asking me to try one short training run. As I attempted to straighten out my stiff knee, the likelihood that I should try to tackle a marathon seemed small. I murmured a quick, questioning prayer under my breath, "Lord, can I really run 26.2 miles on this knee?" No response. I knew there was no way on earth I could cover twenty-six miles that day, but maybe I could endure three miles? It wasn't the end goal that loomed months away in the distance that I needed to focus on. What I needed to do was, by faith, make the choice to run the first few miles. And so I did.

One training run at a time, I chose to focus only on what I had to do that day. Little by little, I chose to get out there and try. On some runs, I felt strong. On other runs, my knee protested, and I had to cut it short. I came across an inspiring quote by the priest Walter Elliott that said, "Perseverance is not a long race; it is many short races one after another." That summed it up for me. To get to where I wanted to be, I had to do what I could today—one run at a time. And that was how God enabled me not only to get through every training run, but also to cross the finish line of the marathon.

THE BEAUTY OF CHOOSING TO ENDURE

We often want to know how something will turn out before we even attempt it. We want guarantees. We want to feel strong before we step out and try. But we don't learn endurance without first showing up—day in and day out—with no guarantees. This is what God is asking of us in this wrestle. In this moment, we don't need to know if we will get to the other side, but we can choose to do whatever it is that God is asking of us today.

We love a victory story, don't we? I can't tell you how often I've flipped on one of those singing competitions on TV and gotten caught up in the emotion of it all. I feel like I am with that young contestant in her moment of glory, bawling as per usual. It's that visceral. "Yes, girl!" You know she has waited such a long time to experience this win. I love watching the one-minute clip about her backstory—how much she had to overcome, how no one thought she would make it, how she had to go it alone, and how she wasn't even sure herself she had what it takes. And then the camera pans to the crowd as they rise to their feet and applaud her last note. She claps her hand over her mouth and tears stream down her face (pan to proud mom and dad hugging each other backstage, also crying). This is her moment, and we love it. We love it for her because we know so well what it feels like to struggle, and we all dream of what that moment of raising our hands in victory must feel like.

But there is something significant that's missing from that one-minute backstory that makes the performer's victory so sweet. What we didn't see were the weeks, months, and years of unsung moments. All the times of trying and failing and wanting to give up. And the truth is, if she hadn't endured through those hard things, she would never have experienced her moment of victory.

All great men and women *learn* endurance. In our "instant"

society where we can get almost anything we want immediately, maybe we have lost sight of the beauty of having to press on and press through, especially when we don't want to. We see people who are where we wish we were, but so often we push back and rebel against the process God has designed to get the blessing He has for us. We would much rather skip the average and ordinary struggles to get to the amazing and extraordinary victories. While it's true that God is a God of miracles, He also requires us to become people who, by His strength, make the choice to get up, show up, and persevere for the blessing that we are wrestling for.

Remember, there is a purpose and an end goal we're aiming for when we choose to endure what seems impossible to endure. We must move in faith and trust that God really does have beauty and blessing and promises to fulfill in our lives. But when we find ourselves in the middle of the wrestle and weary of the fight, we must keep our eyes on the finish line. We do that by focusing on the reason we started this journey to begin with and by looking for the lessons God wants to teach us along the way.

WHEN THE WRESTLE IS LONG

I don't understand why God does the things He does, why He allows the things He allows, or why He chooses the time frames He chooses. I wish I could tell you how your wrestle is going to go, when it will end, and how your circumstances will all work out, but I can't. What I do know is that God has never ceased to be faithful, and you aren't the one person He is going to let slip through the cracks. Holding on to Him will always be worth it, no matter how long it takes.

As I moved through my own wrestling journey, I realized that because it had lasted so long, I began to identify myself with my struggle. When so many days in a row had been hard, I felt that was what defined me—I was the girl with a hard and disappointing life. I resented how long it was taking, and in that resentment, I didn't want to remember all the years God had been faithful. The struggle had become my new normal, and it didn't always feel like it was worth holding on. And this was another hard choice I faced. Would I let my current reality inform my faith?

If I'm honest, I did for a while. Pain is loud like that. But as we endure and hold on to God through our hard days, we must choose not to become identified with our struggles. We must endure as we wrestle and grasp on to truth by choosing to remember everything we have been through with the Lord. We hold on to the hope that, no matter how long this takes, God has something better than we can imagine on the other side of this.

When the wrestle is long, the enemy will tempt you to give up. He will remind you how tired of trying you really are and how nice it might feel to let bitter roots of resentment toward God grow up around your heart. Those roots might feel like they are creating a wall of protection, but they are only there to choke the life out of you and turn your heart away from God.

The enemy has been lying about God's intentions toward humanity since the very beginning. Remember the exchange with Eve in the Garden of Eden? Eve said to the serpent, "God said, 'You shall not eat of the fruit of the tree that is in the midst of the garden, neither shall you touch it, lest you die.' But the serpent said to the woman, 'You will not surely die. For God knows that when you eat of it your eyes will be opened, and you will be like God, knowing good and evil'" (Genesis 3:3-5).

The enemy's deception tactic with Eve is one he still uses today— he wants us to believe we have reason to doubt God's purposes and goodness toward us. Sadly, Eve took the bait and chose to believe that

God was holding out on her and that she would be like God when she ate the fruit. But God had His rules in place to protect her, and the enemy simply took those rules, twisted them, and convinced Eve that God was not worth trusting.

What about you? What are some lies the enemy might be trying to get you to believe in the midst of your wrestle? Are you tempted to believe lies like these?

- I will never get it right, so why even try?
- I am not worthy of what I'm praying for.
- I am unworthy of God's love.
- My life will never change or get better.
- I am alone and no one understands what I'm going through.
- Things will turn out even worse than I'm imagining.
- I might as well give in because I hate my life.
- I will always be rejected.

When the wrestle is long and we are exhausted, we are especially vulnerable to the lies of the enemy. One wrestling quote I came across put it this way: "Take a strong wrestler, get them tired, and they aren't as strong. Take a quick wrestler, get them tired, and they aren't as quick. Take a technical wrestler, get them tired, and they aren't as technical. No matter what kind of wrestler, everyone is afraid of getting tired. It's those who learn to perform when they're tired that find success."[1]

Our weariness makes us easy targets for the enemy. When we are exhausted from trying for so long, we may begin to believe any lie that comes at us. Our hearts are weary of unresolved pain, and so the lies begin to sound like truth. And that's when we can so easily begin to resent and blame the one with whom we wrestle.

When we have been in a long season of endurance and feelings of resentment arise, the best thing we can do is to be honest. The Lord will never reject us for our honesty. Tell Him you need His strength. Tell Him you are beginning to resent Him in this long process. Tell Him you are beginning to believe lies about yourself and Him and ask Him to intervene. Ask Him to give you the ability to endure when you have no strength left and ask Him to bring you the mindset shift you need.

> **When the wrestle is long and we are exhausted, we are especially vulnerable to the lies of the enemy.**

MAKING A MINDSET SHIFT

We now find Jacob at the point in his wrestle when he was in a lot of pain—pain that God Himself had allowed in order to reveal to Jacob how weak he actually was. Despite the pain, Jacob was determined to hold on, even when the Lord asked him to let go: "Then he said, 'Let me go, for the day has broken.' But Jacob said, 'I will not let you go unless you bless me'" (Genesis 32:26).

I believe this marks a mindset shift for Jacob. It was daybreak, the wrestle was meant to end, and the time had come for Jacob to face what he had been fearing—the encounter with his brother, Esau, who Jacob was sure wanted to kill him. Yet, even when he was in possibly the worst pain of his life, Jacob hung on to the one who had wounded him. In that moment, it was no longer about the wrestle but about the one with whom Jacob wrestled. His mind shifted from the struggle he was in to realizing who had come to meet him in that wrestle. He knew this was no ordinary match; he knew God Himself had come to meet him. How was it that he was able to continue in this match while still in so much pain? Was it becoming clear that his strength to endure was because his opponent was enabling him to do so? Realizing this, he was determined to hold on to the Lord until he received what he knew his opponent could give him—a blessing.

When we make the decision to wrestle and dare to endure the hardships we're facing, we come to the point when we realize the purpose of the wrestle was never punishment or the pain, fear, or confusion it brought. The point of the wrestle was to encounter the one who invited us to wrestle in the first place—the one who has been with us in it all along.

God engages us in a wrestle to reveal that there is so much more going on than what we are currently experiencing. His purpose is to reveal Himself to us in a new way. We begin to recognize that all along, it was God Himself that we needed, and that only He can provide the blessing we will walk away with. We begin to see, in a way we never have before, that the one we hold on to with all our endurance is the one who can bring the solutions and change we are so desperate for.

And what does God have for us? What does He want to do for us? What does God want us to know and believe about Him again? Here are just a few of the promises God's Word says we can rely on:

- "[God] is able to do far more abundantly than all that we ask or think, according to the power at work within us" (Ephesians 3:20).
- "[God] is able to keep you from stumbling and to present you blameless before the presence of his glory with great joy" (Jude 1:24).
- "Behold, I am the Lord, the God of all flesh. Is anything too hard for me?" (Jeremiah 32:27).

- "That according to the riches of his glory he may grant you to be strengthened with power through his Spirit in your inner being" (Ephesians 3:16).
- "For nothing will be impossible with God" (Luke 1:37).

Which of these promises apply to you, to your circumstances, to what you want God to do in you and for you and through you?

Some of them?

A few of them?

No, *all* of these promises and so many more apply to you.

It is not wrong to ask the Lord for His blessing. It is a request rooted in faith, an affirmation that you recognize who your Source is. God honors the requests of those who know that it is only by Him, through Him, and because of Him that the path ahead will be better than the path they are on today. Right here, right where you are—broken, burdened, and beside yourself—you can cry out for God's blessing just as Jacob did.

Jacob was weak, weary, and worn out, but he knew that the one with whom he wrestled was the Source who would grant him success and favor in the days to come. He let go of his compulsion to figure everything out himself, and by asking for blessing, he declared he knew God was able. And he did this when he was at his weakest point, crippled by the touch of God. All he had to do was hold on.

Even at our weakest point, we, too, can hold on and ask for the blessing only God can give. We do that when we take our eyes off the wrestle and put them on the one with whom we wrestle.

Imagine how your life might change as you put this into practice. Imagine a life in which you once again see God provide for you in unmistakable ways, where you experience growth and have confidence to move forward because you believe the truth about you and God again. Imagine daring to believe that on the other side of this wrestle and struggle is a faith that is much deeper and far less shakable. As you wrestle, engage the God who loves you unconditionally, and learn to hold on to God while letting go of outcomes, you come to see this is no ordinary scuffle. This is a wrestle for freedom—your freedom and the freedom of those you are called to touch with your life. After this encounter, you may not even recognize yourself, but I can guarantee that you will recognize Jesus.

Friend, the only choice you need to make today is to hold on and do whatever it is God is asking of you in audacious faith. This is endurance. It's choosing to make the tiniest choices you can make today even when you don't know if you have the strength to accomplish some monumental victory later. It might be as simple as putting a Bible verse on your mirror to remind you of truth, going to church when you've been avoiding it, or journaling your pain to process it.

You don't need your own strength; you need His, and He will provide it.

I am confident the Lord has already shown you some small thing He is asking of you or is about to. This step of faith is the choice to continue with endurance. You don't need your own strength; you need His, and He will provide it. If you will just hang on, your small choices to endure will begin to add up and eventually bring the bigger change you long for.

SMALL DAILY CHOICES

Endurance requires faith. We do not know how we are going to get to wherever it is God is taking us. We don't know what it will require of us or how God will provide the strength, but we choose to believe, by faith, that He will provide what we need and that He wants to.

But what does enduring for the blessing really mean? What does it look like for us to say to God, "I will not let go until you bless me"? When we don't yet have proof of the promised blessing in our own lives, we stand on the proof God has already given us.

Because I have been a Christian since I was six, it's easy for Bible verses I learned as a child to feel overly familiar or for me to overlook their gravity and power. But I will tell you, as the Lord began to challenge me more deeply in my wrestle, I had to choose to believe what the Bible said was true, even when I didn't always see how it really mattered. Scripture is not just a big book full of cute quotes that we read on Instagram and pass around on greeting cards. It contains the words of God—and when God speaks, things happen.

Here's another way to think about it. Imagine what it must have been like for Moses after leading God's people out of slavery in Egypt. As he stood at the edge of the Red Sea with Pharaoh's army coming fast behind him, there was no place to go. At that point, he had no personal experience to stand on that God would part the waters to bring them to safety, but he did have God's promise of deliverance, and he moved forward in faith on that promise alone. What miracles might we miss when we don't step out in faith according to God's powerful Word?

When God asks us to endure, we can pray the promises of God's Word back to Him. He spoke these words, and He loves to hear us declare them back to Him in faith. Even when it's hard and you don't really feel like it or believe it will make a difference, I challenge you to pray simple prayers like these over your life.

God is working all of this for my good. "And we know that in all things God works for the good of those who love him, who have been called according to his purpose" (Romans 8:28, NIV).

Lord, please show me glimpses of how you are working all of this for my good. Remind me I am yours and bless me with faith as I dare to believe the good you are working on for me. In Jesus' name, amen.

God will provide strength for me to endure. "So do not fear, for I am with you; do not be dismayed, for I am your God. I will strengthen you and help you; I will uphold you with my righteous right hand" (Isaiah 41:10, NIV).

Lord, please help me not to fear as I walk through this because it is really scary and hard. Bless me with confidence in knowing that you are my God and you promise strength and help. Thank you that when I feel faithless, you are always faithful.

God will show me which next steps to take. "I will instruct you and teach you in the way you should go; I will counsel you with my loving eye on you" (Psalm 32:8, NIV).

Lord, I feel paralyzed and weak. Please show me the small steps I can take and help me to take them. Bless me with your counsel over my life and the awareness that your loving eye is on me. I need you, Lord.

God will give me rest. "Come to me, all you who are weary and burdened, and I will give you rest. Take my yoke upon you and learn from me, for I am gentle and humble in heart, and you will find rest for your souls" (Matthew 11:28-29, NIV).

Lord, you know more than anyone how tired I am of trying. I am weary and burdened by all that I am carrying. Help me to take on your light load and help me to learn from you. Bless me with your gentleness and a humble heart. Through your grace and love, help me to find rest not only for my body, but also for my soul.

God will exchange my anxiety for peace. "Do not be anxious about anything, but in every situation, by prayer and petition, with thanksgiving, present your requests to God. And the peace of God, which transcends all understanding, will guard your hearts and your minds in Christ Jesus. Finally, brothers and sisters, whatever is true, whatever is noble, whatever is right, whatever is pure, whatever is lovely, whatever is admirable—if anything is excellent or praiseworthy—think about such things. Whatever you have learned or received or heard from me, or seen in me—put it into practice. And the God of peace will be with you" (Philippians 4:6-9, NIV).

Lord, you know the anxiety that weighs me down. Give me the faith to believe that I don't need to be anxious about anything. Help me to bring all my needs and requests to you and to thank you as I leave them with you. Bless me with peace that is beyond what I can understand. When I am tempted to focus on all that is wrong and bad, help me to think about what is true, right, lovely, and praiseworthy. Teach me how to practice this and be near me with your peace, Lord.

Choosing to pray God's Word back to Him is an act of faith. And it is one of the small choices you can make to endure. You can decide, despite how hard this season is, that you are going to press on and press through with the Lord. You make the choice to endure every time you choose to both look back at all He has brought you through and to look ahead to all He still wants to do. Some days will feel easier than others, but you can still show up and choose to endure for God's promised blessing.

ONE STEP AT A TIME

If we were to meet in person, I'm guessing you would never look at me and think, *Now, there's a runner.* Even though I may not look the part, and even though I'm not fast, I actually am a runner. I even completed a marathon. I just had to get out there and train by putting one foot in front of the other and praying for endurance.

Practicing is what gets us where we want to be. And practicing is what builds endurance. When it comes to wrestling, "There is no glory in practice, but without practice, there is no glory."[2]

One step, one choice at a time, God is getting you where He wants you. Some steps you take may feel hard and unbearable. Some days, you will walk with ease and maybe even feel like running. Other days, you will wonder if you have made any progress at all and question whether you can continue. But on the good days and the bad, my friend, continue to do the little you can with what you have.

> God is not impatient with your progress. He wants you to see that He is the one who enables you to endure.

Remember, God is not impatient with your progress. He wants you to see that He is the one who enables you to endure.

What is it that makes a blessing or a victory so glorious? Is it the big moment itself, or is it all the little decisions that led up to it? Is it crossing the finish line, or is it the audacious choice to run those first few miles? Is it the accomplishment, or is it knowing in an undeniable way that moment by moment, your God has enabled you to do what you once felt was impossible?

God's Word calls us to our own spiritual race: "Since we are surrounded by so great a cloud of witnesses, let us also lay aside every weight, and sin which clings so closely, and let us run with endurance the race that is set before us" (Hebrews 12:1). And at some point, every follower of Christ will be invited to a wrestle—to struggle with God through their fears and whatever it is that weighs them down. It is through this wrestle that we learn to recognize our weights, throw them off, and endure on the path that God has set before us.

In a world of microwaves, Instant Pots, fast food, and overnight delivery, it can be easy to forget the value of long-haul discipline and perseverance. Finding the endurance to press through in the mundane moments of discouragement and apathy is the fight of faith. It's choosing to believe, despite it all, that God has a blessing He wants to give you—and that it's worth holding on to Him until you get it.

Look at your hand and your five fingers. Every time you feel yourself battling doubt and weariness, tap those five fingers one at a time across the arm of the chair you're in, the sink where you are washing dishes, or the desk where you are working. Say one word with each finger tap, "God, bless me through this."

This is your act of faith and endurance in the middle of the wrestle.

CHALLENGING OLD IDENTITIES

You mustn't confuse a single failure
with a final defeat.
F. SCOTT FITZGERALD,
Tender Is the Night

WHAT IS IT THAT MAKES YOU WHO YOU ARE? What or whom have you asked or even demanded to define you? At some point, we have all looked to something or someone to tell us we are okay and to validate us.

As the Lord pressed me to hold on to Him and I began to change, I discovered that the center of my wrestle was about what I had allowed to define me. God wanted me to break free from all the sources I had relied on to bring me the peace and affirmation that only He could give. He was challenging the source of my identity.

Having grown up in church, I had many times heard the word *identity* and had been told that I needed to find it in Christ. It sounded good and it sounded right, but if I'm honest, I had no clue what that meant. Didn't having my identity in Christ mean doing all the right things, serving Him, and earning the affirmations of those in church leadership? What I began to see was that even good things like these could not replace God as the primary source of my identity.

One way we can immediately identify the sources of our identities is to notice how we react when they're taken away from us.

> **When the sources we have always relied on to tell us we belong, we matter, and we are okay, no longer tell us those things, we quickly become anxious and even desperate.**

When the sources we have always relied on to tell us we belong, we matter, and we are okay no longer tell us those things, we quickly become anxious and even desperate. We may go to great lengths to hold on to those things. We don't know who we are without them because somewhere along the way, we have decided that being "this"—whatever "this" may be—is what brings us worth. As God challenged me, I began to see what He needed me to let go of because of how I reacted when those sources of identity were taken away from me.

IDENTITY IDOLS

Despite the progress I had made, shame continued to attack me because the identity I had carefully crafted for years remained in a million pieces. Up to that point, I hadn't realized that I had based my worth on several outward things, such as what I did for the Lord and saying the "right" things and acting the "right" ways. When I felt like I had nothing left to give, I could no longer earn approval and pats on the back, so there was no longer anyone telling me that I was okay. This lack of approval caused me to experience more cycles of shame. Who was I and what was I worth if I couldn't give and serve and be who people expected me to be? Who *I* expected me to be?

My identity as the "good Christian girl" had become a well-crafted idol, and God was patiently helping me to both recognize that and to let go of it. My heart to serve and do the right things was not bad or wrong. The problem was my need for those I served and admired to respond the way I needed them to for me to feel okay. God was showing me that I was enslaved to the awful taskmasters of performing for God and earning other people's approval.

I loved this idol.

I lived for this idol.

And now, I was dying by this idol—a slow, painful, bitter death of rejection and disapproval. I thought if others wouldn't accept me as broken (because that was all I was), then all I was left with was hate. I hated them, hated me, hated my life and my circumstances. God allowed me to feel the brokenness and the bitterness so I could see how skewed and weak my misplaced identity really was.

THE DANGER OF MISPLACED IDENTITIES

At some point, we all acquire misplaced identities—attachments to the places, people, and things we rely on to tell us that we are okay, worthy, and wanted. When we enter the wrestle, the Lord begins to show us these attachments because when they become idols, they end up owning our hearts and our attention. We will work hard to get approval and acceptance, and we will hate or defend ourselves against anything we perceive to be a threat to that idol.

What misplaced identity might you have crafted for yourself?

- The one who is always willing to help
- The one who is an overachiever
- The one who goes along to get along
- The one who is creative
- The one who leads

- The one who provides advice
- The one who is the life of the party
- The one who serves in all the ministries
- The one who is smart

The list could go on and on. While there's nothing wrong with any of these in and of themselves, the danger comes when we start relying on these identities to tell us we are okay, that we belong, that we are good enough. But what happens to the identity of the caretaker when her own life takes a turn and she can no longer take care of others? What happens to the creative when others consistently reject her ideas or her work? What happens to the achiever who experiences a string of failures? An identity built on something that cannot survive a change in circumstances is an identity that will not stand the test of time. When we hit a hard season, it will fail us.

When we attach our identities to our struggles or our wounds, the growth and healing we need to move on become a threat instead.

The same principle applies when our identities are anchored not to what we do well but to ways we have failed or experienced hardship—when we make an idol of our struggles.

- The one who got a divorce
- The one who is overweight
- The one who struggles with mental health
- The one who battled addiction
- The one who had an abortion
- The one who was cheated on
- The one who was abandoned

- The one who has wayward children
- The one who came from a broken home

When we attach our identities to our struggles or our wounds, the growth and healing we need to move on become a threat instead. The danger is that we do not know who we are outside of the hardship label we have worn for so long. Instead of walking in the freedom Christ died for us to have, we walk enslaved to our pain. And that's no way to live. Take it from Jacob.

WHAT IS YOUR NAME?

When the Lord asked Jacob to let Him go, Jacob responded that he wouldn't let go until the Lord blessed him. And what was the Lord's response to Jacob's request? Instead of giving Jacob an answer, the Lord asked a question.

"And he said to him, 'What is your name?' And he said, 'Jacob'" (Genesis 32:27).

What is your name? What an odd question. The Lord certainly knew Jacob's name. Why would He ask a question to which He already knew the answer? Because it's a characteristically God thing to do.

When God called to Adam after he and Eve had eaten the forbidden fruit, God asked, "Where are you?" (Genesis 3:9).

When God responded to Job's protestations in the face of his suffering, God asked, "Where were you when I laid the foundation of the earth? Tell me, if you have understanding" (Job 38:4).

When Jonah expressed his indignation at God's compassion for Nineveh, God asked, "Do you do well to be angry?" (Jonah 4:4).

When Elijah fled for his life to the wilderness, God asked, "What are you doing here, Elijah?" (1 Kings 19:9).

Asking questions was also something Jesus did.

When Jesus learned a man had been paralyzed for a long time, he asked the man, "Do you want to be healed?" (John 5:6).

When Jesus forgave Peter after Peter denied Him, Jesus asked, "Simon, son of John, do you love me more than these?" (John 21:15).

When a life-threatening storm arose and Jesus' disciples cried out, "Lord, save us! We're going to drown!" Jesus responded, "You of little faith, why are you so afraid?" (Matthew 8:25-26, NIV).

In all these situations, the Lord did not ask the question because He needed an answer; He asked the question because the person He questioned needed the answer. He wanted Adam, Job, Jonah, and all the others to acknowledge what they needed. God asked questions to prompt confession, restore faith, administer correction, prompt reflection, identify desire, and bring restoration.

When God asked Jacob for his name, it was His way of prompting confession. In biblical times, names conveyed the character, personality, or nature of the person. God asked Jacob to confess who he had been—his false identity. And remember, in Hebrew, the name Jacob means "supplanter." In other words, his identity had been that of a schemer and a cheat.

Although Jacob had now asked God to bless him, the behavior that had sent him into exile in the first place was lying and cheating to get Esau's birthright blessing for himself. All those years ago, he had schemed, connived, and lied to get what he wanted, but not this time. This time, God invited him to make a different choice, and He did so by asking a question that required Jacob to reflect on his misplaced identity—who he had been before.

Jacob's life had been defined by his false identity. It drove his choices, his actions, and his interactions. But in this moment, the identity on which he had relied could no longer get him what he wanted. Nor could it alleviate his pain and anxiety. In this stage of the wrestle, he could no longer prevail by force of will, by lying, or by scheming. He was weak and exposed, and God asked a question that required Jacob to peer deeply into the pain of his own soul.

All those years ago, Jacob had lied about his identity to get the blessing he wanted. Would he make a different choice this time?

At some point in our wrestle, God will ask us a question too—and sometimes more than one. As it was with Job, God's questions will require us to peer deeply into the pain of our own souls. He invites us to reflect on who we have been and to exchange who we think we are for who He says we are. This is God's way of not only exposing the identity idols we have looked to for strength and safety, but also of offering us a do-over—a grace-filled chance to make a different choice.

PLEASE VALIDATE ME

As we wrestle through the questions God asks, He reveals and removes whatever it is that has driven us to attach our identities to the wrong things, such as our gifts and skills or our mistakes and wounds. As it was with Jacob, these things have become an expression of our nature. Even though our name might not be "People Pleaser," "Divorcée," or any other false identity name, we always seem to respond when we're called by it.

It was at this point in my wrestle that God revealed my false identity. I wanted to be known as a "good Christian girl," as the "go-to servant," as the "wise one" with biblical advice. That's who I had always relied on myself to be. When I was no longer seen as those things and no longer had anything left to give, I felt my soul arise in indignation. I was furious I could no longer find the validation I was desperate for.

It was during this time that God began to ask many probing questions.

Why the anger?

Why the anxiety?

Why the bitterness?

Why the busyness?

Why the striving?

Why the insecurity?

Ashley, what's at the root of all this?

I was desperately afraid that I was not good enough. I was anxious because I didn't know how to make things better and afraid they were going to get worse. I was bitter because I wanted to be better than I was. I had always considered myself to be strong, and I wanted to be strong again. I stayed busy in the hope that other people would tell me I had value and my life did matter. I lived insecure because no matter what I tried, it failed to give me the validation I needed. I wanted to be good enough, and all I had was proof that I wasn't. The pain of this realization and the way it made me feel exposed was a threat to every ounce of who I was. It was like having an exposed nerve—all I wanted was to escape this excruciating pain.

God asked me these questions and gave me time and space to wrestle through them until I could acknowledge the sources of identity I was relying on that were not Him. It would have been unfaithful and unloving of God to let me continue relying on those idols when what I really needed was Him.

What about you? What reactions have you been living with that might be an indicator of the questions God wants to ask you? He doesn't point them out to shame us but to set us free. We are often so tired and angry with others because we are asking them to give to us what only God can. When these questions trigger emotion or reveal where we may have gotten stuck along the way, we have a choice to make. We can either face the truth of our hurts and let God uproot what needs to be uprooted and replace it with truth, love, and freedom, or we can hold on to our hurts and continue wrestling with Him for control.

I wanted to let go. I wanted to let Him validate me, but I didn't know how. When we have lived in certain patterns of behavior that we believe keep us safe, nothing can be scarier than being exposed over and over to our true need.

I have a clear memory of being in the car with my husband during this time. I felt that familiar agitation in my spirit of knowing I needed to let go of my old identities and yet still feeling driven to rely on them for validation. I felt like my soul was screaming for answers to how I could get my validation itch scratched when I blurted out to my husband, "Tell me, please, what do you think I should do to serve God?" Bubbling just under the surface were thoughts like these: *I just don't want to make the wrong choice. I don't want to do anything for the wrong reasons. I don't want to make God mad. I don't want others to judge me. I want to be okay. Am I good enough? What should I do to feel good enough? Validate me, please.*

Without taking his eyes off the road, he said, "I don't think it matters so much what you do. I don't mind what you do, I care more about who you are and whether you are kind, loving, and happy."

I immediately burst into tears because I knew these weren't just kind words from my husband, but a reminder from God. There was a tenderness to it that reminded me of Jesus' words to Martha when she was frantic and upset, "Martha, Martha, you are anxious and troubled about many things, but one thing is necessary" (Luke 10:41-42). I needed to be reminded that while God cared about what I was going through, He prioritized who I was becoming.

Our culture has trained us to perform for validation and acceptance. That's why so many of us are tempted every day to post something on social media—we crave immediate affirmation in the form of likes and follows. *Am I good enough? Do you like me? Validate me, please.* When God no longer allows us to run to these false sources of identity to bring us security and worth, He does so to set us free, even though it hurts. We cannot continue to rely on these sources to tell us who we truly are and to give us what we truly need. God loves us and calls us worthy because we are His children.

> One of the bravest things God may ever ask us to do is to trust Him when the questions are hard, our nerves are exposed, and what we have been avoiding or denying for so long is dragged into the light.

One of the bravest things God may ever ask us to do is to trust Him when the questions are hard, our nerves are exposed, and what we have been avoiding or denying for so long is dragged into the light. Rather than doing the easy fix of bailing us out of our misery, God wants us to trust that doing the difficult inner work in our hearts is what matters most.

If you're like me, you may know what God is inviting you to face but you aren't sure you are ready to address it. What does it mean in practical terms to let God do what He has come to do in this wrestling season? While I can't tell you the details of what that process might require of you, I can give you a peek into my heart and mind by sharing something I wrote in my journal as I entered this uprooting season in my own life.

I have always had this sense that I need to "hurry up and be better." Perhaps I think of my brokenness as a burden, my processing of pain as annoying, and so I need to hurry up past this imperfection to become easier for both myself and others.

But I am so overly aware that this is not a race. I am not going to wake up today, tomorrow, or even the next day and be whole, healed, or ready, no matter how much I wish I could be. And this is where I am changing—changing my thinking and my response to myself.

It comes down to a choice, and I choose to allow God to be my best friend, my cheerleader, my encourager, and to learn to offer grace to myself instead of hatred. I can tell myself things like . . .

"It's okay to cry about that."

"It's okay to feel that and hurt about that."

"Take your time."

"Your beauty is far deeper than your appearance."

"It's okay to love yourself and find beauty in yourself and be nice to yourself because Jesus does too."

I am constantly thinking about how I can't control what others think of me, but I can control what I think. If they choose to hate me, judge me, or criticize me—well, that is their problem and their issue. I am aware that my own issues are big enough to fill my hands without having to control or worry about other people's issues too.

I can choose to believe God, to be kinder to myself, to be brave, and to no longer be controlled by guilt or fear. I can choose to stand up in who I am, in who God says I am, and to take the time to figure out who that is.

Allowing God to love me and show me how He loves me is making this change in me. He is here, walking with me, helping me, and wiping away every tear. He is holding my hand every step of the way. He is never in a hurry; He just lets me be, reminding me all the while that healing doesn't happen overnight. I sense Him urging me to be patient with myself, telling me I don't have the ability or resources to heal myself, but He does.

Never in my life have these words been so real to me: "My strength is made perfect in weakness" (2 Corinthians 12:9, NKJV).

When I start to feel like I am drowning again and those old feelings of being trapped and stuck and hopeless come, I tell Him, "Lord, I have no idea what to do! Don't let me go back there. Please help." And He does!

I feel broken open, like when the roots of a tooth are exposed. The pain is sharp. Yet, every day the Lord takes me a little farther and replaces the lies that I believed for so long with truth.

I feel a fight in me today, a renewed energy. Renewal of my mind is happening. I choose to think different thoughts about myself and different thoughts about others, even strangers. I am desperate for the mind of Christ and hanging on to Him for hope and freedom. I am so aware that this is not going to happen without His miraculous help.

And He is doing miraculous healing in me. My sister and my husband have given me the greatest compliment—they see I am changing. Glory to the Lord!

I am making different choices now. I have a perspective and an understanding that I didn't have before. Slowly, I will become who God says I am. I will let go of who I think I am supposed to be and just be me. I will find a way to love myself even when I am not perfect. I can work toward being a better me in mind, body, and spirit—not by hating myself into perfection, but by loving myself into progress. This is how God works with me—with all of us. And I will honor Him by doing the same.

Glorify yourself through my healing, Lord.

And friend, He did.

One month, one day, one step, and one thought at a time, the Lord began to release me, heal me, and help me to embrace the identity that is truly mine in Christ. Are there days when I still struggle, when I still need to look back on what God says about me and let go of the identities I once demanded tell me who I am? Absolutely. But when I lean on God's strength, it functions like a muscle—my ability to lean gets stronger with use, which means it also gets easier. What once required effort and time now happens much more quickly.

CONFESSION AND REPENTANCE

As God revealed my misplaced identity and what I had believed about myself, He also called me to confession and repentance. Confession is simply the admission that we have been wrong. In my case, I had been relying on who I thought I should be instead of relying on who God said I was. I had been trusting that those lies were true rather than choosing to trust the Word of God, despite my circumstances. I wanted to confess and repent, not to be religious but to be restored. I admitted to God that I had been off track in my thinking and that I wanted to return to the place He was calling me—to truth and freedom.

Just as God asked Jacob to reckon with what his identity had been, God asks us to name the misplaced identities we are ready and willing to let go of now that they have been brought to our attention. And if the thought of that sounds scary, consider what God's Word says about confession and repentance:

> Repent, then, and turn to God, so that your sins may be wiped out, that times of refreshing may come from the Lord.
> **ACTS 3:19, NIV**

> For when I kept silent, my bones wasted away through my groaning all day long. For day and night your hand was heavy upon me; my strength was dried up as by the heat of summer. I acknowledged my sin to you, and I did not cover my iniquity; I said, "I will confess my transgressions to the LORD," and you forgave the iniquity of my sin. . . . You are a hiding place for me; you preserve me from trouble; you surround me with shouts of deliverance.
> **PSALM 32:3-5, 7**

> Those whom I love, I reprove and discipline, so be zealous and repent.
> **REVELATION 3:19**

In all three of these Scriptures, we see the good things that come from confession and repentance: a time of refreshing, deliverance, and proof of God's love. God doesn't call us to repentance because He needs to hear it but so He can bring us the blessings of truth and freedom—the refreshment our souls desperately need.

CLINGING TO THE SAVIOR

Those that resolve, though God slay them,
yet to trust in him, will, at length,
be more than conquerors.
MATTHEW HENRY,
Matthew Henry's Commentary

I RECENTLY ATTENDED MY FIRST SEDER, the ritual feast at the beginning of Passover. Passover is the Jewish holiday that celebrates the exodus of God's people from slavery in Egypt. One of the customs is to take bitter herbs, dip them in salt water, and eat them. Eating bitter herbs commemorates the bitter tears of the Jewish people as they cried to God in their slavery, and how the Lord heard their pleas for rescue:

> The LORD said, "I have indeed seen the misery of my people in Egypt. I have heard them crying out because of their slave drivers, and I am concerned about their suffering."
> **EXODUS 3:7, NIV**

I am sure you have your own story of many bitter tears. While I can't begin to imagine what you are walking through right now and all the ways you are holding on for dear life to your precious Savior, I can promise you this: He sees your misery and hears your pleas for rescue. He has compassion for you and is concerned about your suffering. He knows the darkness of facing pain when there seems to be no way out. He also sees more than you ever could. He understands the entirety of your story—and you will one day understand it too if you trust Him through your difficulties and dark days.

The Seder was a profound experience of remembering how God miraculously rescued His people, providing a way out of the suffering they were desperate to escape and leading them to the Promised Land He had prepared for them. It was also a reminder that the blessing of freedom didn't play out as the Israelites expected it to. Their deliverance was long, hard, and confusing. God could have taken them directly to the Promised Land, an eleven-day journey, but instead, He led them through a season of wandering in the desert.

> When Pharaoh let the people go, God did not lead them by way of the land of the Philistines, *although that was near*. For God said, "Lest the people change their minds when they see war and return to Egypt." But God led the people around by the way of the wilderness toward the Red Sea. And the people of Israel went up out of the land of Egypt equipped for battle.
>
> EXODUS 13:17-18, emphasis added

God knows how easily we might change our minds when we see the battles ahead—what we will have to face and overcome to be free. That's when we start to reason that maybe we don't really want to be free after all. He knows that sometimes He has to lead us down an unexpected path to get us where He wants us to be, because *He is concerned not only about where we are going, but also about who we are becoming.*

It's probably no surprise to you that God's way of doing things is not always the way we would do them. He doesn't take His cues from our will, our patterns, or our plans. Instead, He often takes an inverse approach, doing the opposite of what we might expect.

> We trust God and let go of outcomes because we know the blessing we seek will likely come in a way we can't imagine or expect.

To be the greatest we must become the least (Matthew 20:25-28).

To be exalted we must humble ourselves (Matthew 23:12).

To be perfect we must love our enemies rather than hate them (Matthew 5:43-48).

To find our lives we must first lose them (Matthew 16:24-25).

And to be freed from our struggles and pain, we must make the choice to wrestle through them. We trust God and let go of outcomes because we know the blessing we seek will likely come in a way we can't imagine or expect.

I know it doesn't make sense. I know it feels backward. I know you probably wish with all your heart that there was another way, but you can trust Him in this process. God knows what He is doing, and He knows who you are becoming—just as He knew who Jacob was becoming.

THE BLESSING OF A NEW NAME

We're at the point in Jacob's story where Jacob has demanded a blessing and the Lord has responded by asking Jacob his name. It was the Lord's way of inviting Jacob to acknowledge the truth of who he had been. The next intriguing turn of events happened after Jacob stated his name and the Lord responded, "Your name shall no longer be called Jacob, but Israel, for you have striven with God and with men, and have prevailed" (Genesis 32:28).

Wait, a new name? Why a new name?

To answer that question, it's important to know some background. In those days, the ability to confer a new name on someone was a mark of authority—the one conferring the new name had authority over the one who received the new name. We see this when Daniel and his three friends were exiled to Babylon.

> And the chief of the eunuchs gave them names: Daniel he
> called Belteshazzar, Hananiah he called Shadrach, Mishael
> he called Meshach, and Azariah he called Abednego.
> DANIEL 1:7

Scholars also point out that in biblical times, names weren't neutral in the way they are today. Instead, names were an indication of character as well as a reflection of one's beliefs or past. Because Daniel and his friends had been taken captive, the Babylonians didn't want these four young men to identify with who they had been in their Hebrew past; they wanted them to become Babylonian and conform to Babylonian ways of living. Therefore, the first order of business was a name change. As their captors, the Babylonians had the right and authority to do this.

From Genesis to Revelation, we see examples of God changing names. From Abram to Abraham, Sarai to Sarah, Simon to Peter, and Saul to Paul, God exerted His authority over their identities as they walked with Him and moved toward who He had created and called them to be. And God's authority to change names isn't just a thing of the past. Scripture promises that God has a new name for you and me as well.

> To the one who conquers I will give some of the hidden manna, and I will give him a white stone, with a new name written on the stone that no one knows except the one who receives it.
> REVELATION 2:17

Talk about wild stuff! A white rock with a new name on it that only the one who receives it will know? Why? What could be the reason for this?

Here's how theologian William MacDonald explains it:

> The white stone has been explained in many ways. It was a token of acquittal in a legal case. It was a symbol of victory in an athletic contest. It was an expression of welcome given by a host to his guest. It seems clear that it is a reward given by the Lord to the overcomer and expressing individual approval by Him. . . . the new name indicates acceptance by God and title to glory.[1]

I don't pretend to understand what all of this might entail, but this much seems clear: We who wrestle in life and overcome receive a new name that declares both our victory over our suffering and our new identities as conquerors.

When God conferred a new name on Jacob, it was an acknowledgment that Jacob had struggled and overcome but also an acknowledgement of God's authority. Through Jacob's struggle with God, he was transformed into the man God had called him to be and always intended him to be.

Here is how various Bible versions translate the Lord's explanation for Jacob's name change in Genesis 32:28:

"You have *striven* with God and with men, and have prevailed" (ESV).

"You have *struggled* with God and with humans and have overcome" (NIV).

"You have *fought* with God and with men and have won" (NLT).

"You have *contended* with God and with men, and have prevailed" (NASB).

"You've *wrestled* with God and you've come through" (MSG).

Jacob had striven, struggled, fought, contended, and, yes, wrestled with God—and he came through. In the process, he was transformed to the point that he could no longer be called by a name that identified him with his past.

One Bible commentary describes the meaning of the name Israel as "perseverer with God."[2] What a different shift that puts on it! Instead of being known as Jacob, a schemer and a cheat, he would be known as Israel, one who persevered with God. Now, whenever he was called by his new name, Israel would be reminded of how God viewed him and who God called him to be. One who perseveres with God.

> **We are conquerors every time we hold on to God even when we don't feel like we have what it takes to keep going.**

The same can be true of you and me. When we persevere with God, we become conquerors. We are conquerors when we choose to die to our ways and our demands. We are conquerors when we let go of outcomes and having to understand all the whys. We are conquerors when we lift our hands in praise and choose to trust our God even when life hurts. We are conquerors every time we hold on to God even when we don't feel like we have what it takes to keep going.

That's how the wrestle results in the blessing of personal transformation. The way to the blessing, to becoming more like Christ, is through the trials we face. When the only thing we can do is hold on and trust God when it hurts the most, we persevere in the knowledge that He is focused on who we are becoming—our new, more Christlike identity.

The truth is, if we could choose out of a box all the things that would happen in our lives, we would never choose any of our past or current struggles. Never. But without those things, we might never get to the root of our problems, the truth of what we really believe, and all the ways we say we trust God but don't. We can't grow or become who God has created us to be without the wrestle. And God in His faithfulness will bring this blessing into our lives. The only question is, Will we surrender to the authority of our good God as He is faithful to change us?

It was through holding on, through pain, and through persevering that the Lord blessed Jacob with what he really needed—a new identity. But there was more to come.

Once the Lord had given Jacob a new name, there is this intriguing exchange between them:

> Then Jacob asked him, "Please tell me your name." But he said, "Why is it that you ask my name?" And there he blessed him.
> GENESIS 32:29

It seems that a little bit of Jacob's old nature was still active. Having surrendered to the Lord's authority by accepting his new name, Jacob nevertheless made one last attempt to exert some control by asking for his opponent's name. And once again, the Lord responded by asking a question. Remember, God never asks a question because He needs an answer; He asks a question because the person He questions needs an answer. Just as God had asked Jacob his name to help him face his past identity, God again asked a question to redirect Jacob to his new identity—an identity in which he lived under God's authority.

Like Jacob, we have our own questions that persist throughout our struggles, perhaps the biggest and scariest of which is just one word, *Why?* But sometimes God chooses not to answer those questions, at least not directly. And yet, He still releases the blessing of the wrestle in our lives. Perhaps God saw Jacob's question for what it was—one last attempt to regain some power and control. Jacob already knew the name of the one with whom he wrestled. Now, he just had to receive the blessing of being under God's authority and, by faith, take his next step into an unknown future.

Will we do the same?

THE PROMISE OF ENDURANCE

The other day in my small group, a passage I have read many times struck me in a new way. I love it when this happens! The passage was in Romans 8, and I highly recommend reading the entire chapter when you get a chance. There's so much good stuff in there about life in the Spirit, our present suffering and future glory, how we are more than conquerors, and how nothing can separate us from God's love.

All of these themes are not only encouraging but especially relevant when we are tired of trying and it seems like the struggle will never end. Here is the verse that initially caught my attention when I read it in my small group:

> For I consider that the sufferings of this present time are not worth comparing with the glory that is to be revealed to us.
> **ROMANS 8:18**

Paul's words reminded me of this description of Jesus: "who for the joy that was set before him endured the cross" (Hebrews 12:2). It stood out to me because so often I want my joy to be now; I want to see the glory revealed in this moment. But sometimes joy is what lies ahead. For the time being, it is held in hope so we can experience it on the other side of our enduring. This is how, like Jacob, we become perseverers with God—we endure by focusing on the joy or the blessing ahead.

Paul continues:

> Now hope that is seen is not hope. For who hopes for what he sees? But if we hope for what we do not see, we wait for it with patience.
>
> Likewise the Spirit helps us in our weakness. For we do not know what to pray for as we ought, but the Spirit himself intercedes for us with groanings too deep for words. And he who searches hearts knows what is the mind of the Spirit, because the Spirit intercedes for the saints according to the will of God. And we know that for those who love God all things work together for good, for those who are called according to his purpose.
>
> ROMANS 8:24-28

God's intent in our sufferings is to work them together for good, but Paul also clearly says that we have to wait with patience for God to do what He is going to do. To hope is to make the choice to wait and to trust. God knows that this is a hard choice. He knows we are weak, especially when we feel tired of trying, and so He helps us. The Holy Spirit intercedes for us according to the will of God! Let that sink in for a minute, friend. These are the words of God.

These are the words you can stand on when you are tired of waiting with patience.

These are the words you can declare when you don't see how things could possibly work together for good.

These are the words you can believe by faith when you don't know what to say, what to do, or where to go, because the Holy Spirit is praying on your behalf according to God's will.

We are not the faithful ones, He is. This wrestle is His plan and it's His job, as we put our hope in Him, to get us to the other side of this. And sometimes it's in the middle of waiting patiently for the good God is working that we discover God Himself is all we ever really needed. God alone—not everything working out the way we want—is our hope. We don't have to wait for anything in our circumstances to change to experience Him right here, right now, in this very moment. In fact, that is one of the marks of transformation—realizing that the greatest blessing is always the Blesser.

Read on as Paul gives us the rallying cry we need to hear again and again when we are struggling. Imagine he wrote these words directly to you, knowing your pain, your unanswered questions, how tired your soul is, and the long wait you are enduring.

> What then shall we say to these things? If God is for us, who
> can be against us? He who did not spare his own Son but gave
> him up for us all, how will he not also with him graciously give
> us all things? Who shall bring any charge against God's elect?
> It is God who justifies. Who is to condemn? Christ Jesus is
> the one who died—more than that, who was raised—who is at
> the right hand of God, who indeed is interceding for us. Who

shall separate us from the love of Christ? Shall tribulation, or distress, or persecution, or famine, or nakedness, or danger, or sword? As it is written,

"For your sake we are being killed all the day long;
    we are regarded as sheep to be slaughtered."

No, in all these things we are more than conquerors through him who loved us. For I am sure that neither death nor life, nor angels nor rulers, nor things present nor things to come, nor powers, nor height nor depth, nor anything else in all creation, will be able to separate us from the love of God in Christ Jesus our Lord.

ROMANS 8:31-39, emphasis added

Come on, somebody! That definitely deserves an amen!

We *are* more than conquerors through Him who loved us. As we hold on to Him and wait for our promised blessing, we will overcome. What does it look like to hold on until God blesses us? Here is how I described it as I walked through my own season of pain.

I can almost imagine Jesus chasing me with His love saying, "Here I am. I died to save you, let me save you, I will save you."

I wanted my family to understand me and see me and tell me my life was worth something and not be irritated or annoyed with me. I wanted my church friends and staff to offer me some magical solution that would make me better. If I served them long enough and hard enough, I hoped that I would somehow feel better. But He didn't want any of that from me. All of it was so shallow, so empty, so temporary.

Jesus allowed me to get to a point where I was—and am—desperate for a Savior. My deepest cry was for someone to save me, and I knew the only real answer was Him. He didn't want me to serve Him, to be "perfect," act "right," be more like some "super Christian." He loved me just the way I was and wanted me to let Him love me.

Even when I wasn't reading my Bible for an hour a day and couldn't bring myself to pray, even when I stopped serving in any capacity at church, He wanted me to know that I was still worth loving. There was nothing I could do or say or be "more of" for Him to want to save me and set me free. He wanted to show me the prison I sat in and that He was coming to save me. He's the only one who could.

He and I are in that process now, and I have learned that the only way I will find out who I am is to be close enough to Him to see myself through His eyes.

He showed me the labels I gave myself. The labels in which I once found comfort and purpose were superficial and just that—labels. We are walking through this at this very moment, and while I still look through the clouded lenses of my own self-doubt, I am trying to learn once again that He is the beauty and worth in me.

He is not in a hurry with me. He has given me the power to be more than a conqueror, and He is teaching me once again to tell the enemy to shut up, because I know who I am in Him. I am His.

Jesus has been fighting for me all this time, and He is teaching me how to be a fighter again and how to stand in

His authority. He is teaching me to believe that even when people fail me, He never will. He is showing me that if I am okay with Him, it doesn't matter whether anyone else approves of me or gives me recognition or validates my worth, because I only need Jesus.

I know this journey is far from over, and I know my dependence on Him through it is vital, but I trust He is leading me to full freedom. Through His truth and love, I will become the person He needs me to be to tell others about this Savior we so desperately need, even after we've been "saved."

There is no formula for your walk with God, but you can choose to audaciously hold on to God while you wrestle and He reveals who He is, why He can be trusted, and how He is blessing you and bringing more and more freedom. You can choose to believe day in and day out that God is good and He will get you through this. You can choose to dig through the ashes until you see the beauty and the lessons underneath. Those ashes are the soil in which God plants renewed faith in you, helping you to remember all He has for you. Your wrestle with God is just part of your story, not the end of your story. Your wrestle is preparing you for the beautiful and meaningful future God has for you.

So what do we do to endure? We do all those things I just mentioned:

- We resolve to hold on to God no matter how bad our circumstances get.
- We make a choice to set our minds on the things God is doing now and not just on what He has yet to do.

- We listen for what God is saying and look for what He is revealing to us in this time.
- We notice the changes we begin to see in ourselves as the blessing of transformation takes root in us.

Conquerors become conquerors by fighting. Overcomers become overcomers by persevering. Warriors become warriors by staying in the battle through both the pain of defeat and the amazing glory of victory. And this, my friend, requires making these choices to endure every day.

You have no idea what this season of wrestling may be preparing you for in the future and the way God needs you to know Him and stand in faith for yourself and others.

THE BEAUTY OF PREPARATION

The hardest choice I ever had to make was the choice to accept God's invitation to the wrestle. I decided that if He was asking me to wrestle with Him in this season, I would do it. I would be all in and put everything I had into walking through it with Him. The months and years that followed were some of the hardest and loneliest I had ever faced. And one particularly hard day was the day of my baby shower for my second son.

I was sitting in my mom's living room with a friend I had picked up and brought with me. My mom knew how little money we had to support this new baby and had gone out of her way to make it a special occasion. There were little mason jars filled with pink lemonade and topped with green-and-white-striped straws and handmade banners with my son's name. Most of the beautifully wrapped presents were from her as well.

Over the previous few weeks, I had both emailed and hand-delivered invitations to friends to invite them to the shower, but no one RSVP'd. As the three of us sat there occasionally glancing at the door, the start time for the shower came and went. No one else ever showed up.

Pain intruded into my heart as I thought back fondly to my home church and my first baby shower where I had so many friends I could hardly fit them all into one room. And now, this? All the cute mason jar cups of lemonade sat lined up on the sink, untouched.

I felt humiliated and so vulnerable. I appreciated the gifts and the love I did receive that day, but it was another hit to my bruised soul and a temptation to welcome back those self-defeating inner voices. *You're a joke. How does it feel to be rejected even when you're pregnant?*

Yet, somehow through this process, as I learned to look for what God was doing, I knew what God was asking of me, which was to endure and persevere through this pain. Knowing this didn't make it hurt any less, but I was comforted as I sensed He was speaking to my spirit, "Remain, Ashley. I am enough for you, even in this."

Might we dare to believe that even in our pain, God is still loving us best? That when we are obedient to whatever God requires of us in the moment, He is in fact positioning us for the blessing He has prepared for us?

During my wrestling season, there were times that obedience to what God required of me in the moment was something as simple as doing the dishes. Truth be told, there were days I felt so sad and exhausted that I would have told you I wasn't capable of even that. But day by day, when I felt that nudge from God to do the smallest task He placed before me, I did my best to obey. Whether it was the dishes, apologizing to my husband for yelling at him for no good reason (again), or meditating on Scripture verses God brought to my heart and mind, I chose to believe He was asking me to trust His preparation process in the small things.

That's what endurance is—the choice to keep showing up and doing the thing right in front of us, day in and day out. God can use even the seemingly monotonous tasks of our lives as part of a season of preparation. And preparation is all about positioning us for the blessing God has prepared. Seasons of endurance are just as much part of our journeys as doing the next, better, more important thing, whatever that may be. It is all in the way we choose to see it.

> **G**od can use even the seemingly monotonous tasks of our lives as part of a season of preparation. And preparation is all about positioning us for the blessing God has prepared.

The Israelites wandered in the wilderness, David watched sheep, Jacob wrestled with God. All these experiences had the same purpose—to establish who our Source is and how very dependent we are on Him. God allows us to see our own weaknesses and what is truly in our hearts so we can understand that when we surrender to His authority, we become who He is changing us into. That's how He gives us a new name and helps us walk in our new and true identity.

YOUR TRUE NAME

My son's name is Eisy (pronounced eee-sigh). We named him after my husband's middle name. To be sure, it's an unusual name, and my son has to deal with people mispronouncing it all the time.

When we moved into our new house after moving across the country, Eisy began to meet the neighbors. One day, the little boy from across the street came over and knocked on our door to ask if "Ethan" could play. I just assumed he had gotten Eisy's name wrong and sent them out to play. When I asked Eisy about it later, he said, "Yeah, I just told him my name was Ethan." Now every time we pass our neighbors, they say, "Hi, Ethan!"

As his mom, it makes me both laugh and want him to correct his little friend. Although Ethan is a fine name, it's not my son's name. I want him to·be known for who he really is. There is so much about my son that fits his name: his wild imagination, his fancy dance moves, and his sensitive heart.

The one who chose our names wants us to be known for who we really are as well. For too long we have gone by names that are not our own because we have told people, or allowed people to tell us, what our names are: overlooked, unworthy, not enough, too much, gross, overly emotional, too quiet, and the list could go on and on. But those aren't our names, and as we wrestle, the Lord wants us to know our true names and to live in the truth of who we really are.

We're blessed, but we're not done yet. As we move from the season of struggling with God into receiving God's blessing, we need to tackle the areas in which we have been stuck and let God move us on and challenge us to trust Him with our whole hearts again.

And just as a reminder, you're not Ethan.

PART 3

THE BLESSINGS
OF BEING BROKEN

BLESSED TO REBUILD TRUST

Only you can decide how your fires will affect you.
Will you be sanctified or scarred?
BETH MOORE,
A Woman's Heart

THERE COMES A POINT IN OUR WRESTLE with God when we make the choice to trust Him again. When I reached this point, I was still very broken, but I was willing to think new thoughts and dare to walk by faith again. As I held on to God for the blessing, I began to see what He was doing. Bible verses I had known all my life suddenly took on new meaning because I was now living them in a way I never had before.

I also knew that if I was going to do this faith and trust thing, then I needed to be all in. And to do that, I needed outside help. I emailed my church, and they connected me with a woman named Sarah who was studying soul care at a local seminary. She agreed to meet with me.

I was both excited and scared to take this step. I was still desperate for relief, but so many things had gone wrong so many times that it was hard not to wonder if I was just setting myself up for still more hard things to come. *What if this doesn't help? What if I try it and nothing changes? What if I end up with more pain?*

Taking a risk to trust again absolutely requires vulnerability.

The first time I met with Sarah, I followed her down a flight of stairs to her basement apartment and sat on her couch. She lit a candle, which smelled so nice, said a brief prayer, and then simply asked me to tell her what was going on.

As I began to speak, tears rolled down my cheeks. I felt so lost and so afraid of the darkness in my heart. When she asked me what I did to spend time with God, I acknowledged that I didn't do much these days, but when things had been much better, I could easily read the Bible and write in my prayer journal for an hour a day. As soon as the words left my lips, I felt shame wash over me. I believed if I really loved God like I said I did, I would have found a way to spend that time with Him.

Taking a risk to trust again absolutely requires vulnerability.

Sometimes God brings people into our lives to show us His heart for us, and to release us from the very things that have caused us to doubt His love and care for us. That's who Sarah was for me. She looked at me with compassion and said, "Maybe you need to stop trying so hard and just let God minister to you. Maybe you need to receive from Him."

"What do you mean by 'receive' from Him?" I asked.

"The next time you spend time with God, try taking this position," she said. She held out her hands in front of her with her palms facing up as if she were waiting to receive a gift. "Let this season be about what God wants to give to you and about being open and willing to receive it."

I could feel the old me, the person God had been wrestling with, bristle. How would I prove I was a "good" Christian without checking all my devotional-time boxes? Faces of those from my past who had been particularly religious popped into my mind and shook their heads in disapproval.

But as the tears continued to stream down my face, I knew I needed to be willing to let go of my fears of being wrong or not performing in the right way. I was tired of believing God was disappointed in me, and I wanted to trust Him again. *What if the best way to do that was to learn to receive from Him? What would He give me? What did I want from Him? What would He tell me?*

As I later reflected on what Sarah had said, I began to imagine myself sitting in the middle of my ashes. In the past, I had imagined the Lord standing over me with His arms crossed, tapping His holy toe, waiting impatiently for me to get myself together. Now, I imagined Him sitting in the ashes with me. Instead of speaking words of condemnation or hurry, He was gentle and patient. I felt like He would sit there with me for as long as it took for me to believe that He loved me just as much when I was crawling and had nothing to offer, as when I was running and slaying giants.

That's when I realized my own role in undermining trust with my Savior. The thing about trust is, it can't happen without honesty. Think about it. How can you have intimacy and trust that someone really loves you if you're always putting on an act and trying to be who you think they want you to be? It's exhausting because you know it's not true. And you're afraid of what might happen if they find out you don't always act, look, or feel like they have always seen you—will they still love you?

Jesus had seen the real me, of course, but I had chosen to distance myself from Him every time I couldn't keep up the act, only returning when I felt like I could get it together enough to be acceptable again. Learning to trust that He loved me even when I had nothing to give was a whole new stage of the wrestle.

My heart broke open just a little bit that day as Sarah challenged me this way. And little by little, God spoke to me through sermons, songs, and quiet moments that brought healing to my heart in a way only He knew I needed.

What might choosing to trust God again require of you? As you emerge from your own wrestling season, perhaps you are scared about what the future holds. You may be uncertain of how God feels about you and unsure of how you feel about Him. Perhaps you still worry about your doubts. Maybe you are still dealing with pain and aren't sure how you will ever heal. Wherever you find yourself, will you dare to trust Him again? Perhaps God has brought you to this place to give you a blessing you could have no other way. Will you take the risk of holding out your hands with an expectation to receive from Him, even if you have nothing to give?

The promise of Scripture is, "We love, because He first loved us" (1 John 4:19, NASB). What Scripture doesn't say is, "We love because we're supposed to" or "We love so that God will love us." No, before we were even thinking about loving or pleasing God, He died on a cross for us. He has always been the one who loved first. Why would this time with you be any different? Yes, opening yourself to receive from God and to let Him love you may feel risky, but I can promise you that it will be worth it.

REBUILDING TRUST WITH OTHERS

When we've been struggling for a long time, it can be hard to untangle our mistrust of God from our mistrust of well-meaning people who may have intended to make us feel better but too often ended up making us feel worse.

When we're hurting, what we really need is someone who will listen and allow us to process the deep pain we're struggling with. When they instead shove Bible verses toward us in the hope that verses will fix us, even the truth of God's Word can become a resentment point.

People mean well, don't they? I think for the most part they do. It's human nature to want to help when we see someone having a hard time. But too often, instead of listening to us and letting us be in our pain, people try to hustle us through it by offering quick-fix Bible sound bites. Instead of offering us empathy, they offer us sympathy.

Author Brené Brown describes why that's a problem: "Empathy fuels connection and sympathy drives disconnection."[1] She goes on to say that when we share something painful and someone responds with an "at least" statement, they minimize our pain by trying to paint a silver lining around it. For example:

"I had a miscarriage." "At least you know you can get pregnant."

"I think my marriage is falling apart." "At least you have a marriage."

"John's getting kicked out of school." "At least Sarah is an A-student!"[2]

In the Christian world, the "at least" statements might sound like this:

"I had a miscarriage." "At least God is still good."

"I think my marriage is falling apart." "At least God will work all things together for good."

"John's getting kicked out of school." "At least God knows the plans He has for you. Plans to prosper you and not to harm you."

People who offer us sympathy mean well, and I confess I've said my own share of "at least" statements over the years. It seems like a way to bring hope, right? That doesn't mean we shouldn't encourage one another with truth—of course we should. Truth stands and doesn't change. But sometimes we use these statements to avoid the discomfort of empathy—of being with someone in their pain. It's so much easier to quote a Bible verse, promise to pray, and wish them well.

When all we get is sympathy and our pain goes unheard or acknowledged, we shame ourselves for not having enough faith or not being willing to look on that bright side of hope. When we keep trying to digest truth that's delivered as sympathy, we eventually begin to resent it because it hurts. In fact, it cuts more deeply because what it communicates is that struggling on this level is somehow wrong and maybe even ungodly. And what do we do with that when we're already beat down?

As part of rebuilding trust with God, we also need to find at least one other person who will enter into our story with empathy. Someone who is willing to be with us in our hardest and darkest moments and say, "I'm so sorry," or even just to be with us without saying much of anything at all.

Not long ago, I came across a video on social media that struck me as a beautiful illustration of this. A woman was lying on her driveway in the rain. It seemed clear that she was struggling. Then a car drove by, backed up, and parked. When the woman in the car recognized her friend, she immediately hopped out of the car and laid down next to her hurting friend in the pouring rain. I think every soul craves a friend who is willing to lie down next to us when we find ourselves in a drenching rain, the kind of friend who never hustles us along with Bible sound bites or makes us feel like we need to "hurry up and get over it."

> We can let people off the hook for not being able to be God to us.

If you have felt mistreated, misunderstood, or misrepresented by God's people, will you dare to let go of any pain they may have caused you with the same grace you know you also need when you unintentionally harm people? Finding freedom always involves forgiveness, and this whole journey was never about them anyway. We can let people off the hook for not being able to be God to us.

REBUILD TRUST THROUGH HONESTY

I don't know where we get the idea that we can't be honest with God about our struggles and how we are feeling. That's definitely not what the Bible teaches. In fact, the Bible includes a whole book of prayers that contain every emotion, from the pits of despair to the heights of ecstatic praise. And many of them were written by David, a man who knew how to be honest with God.

Let's take a look at just a few of the many honest prayers David prayed:

- "Give ear to my words, O LORD; consider my groaning" (Psalm 5:1).
- "Be gracious to me, O LORD, for I am languishing; heal me, O LORD, for my bones are troubled. My soul also is greatly troubled. But you, O LORD—how long? . . . I am weary with my moaning; every night I flood my bed with tears; I drench my couch with my weeping. My eye wastes away because of grief; it grows weak because of all my foes" (Psalm 6:2-3, 6-7).
- "Why, O Lord, do you stand far away? Why do you hide yourself in times of trouble?" (Psalm 10:1).
- "How long, O LORD? Will you forget me forever? How long will you hide your face from me?" (Psalm 13:1).
- "Turn to me and be gracious to me, for I am lonely and afflicted. The troubles of my heart are enlarged; bring me out of my distresses. Consider my affliction and my trouble, and forgive all my sins" (Psalm 25:16-18).

It's clear from David's prayers that he was not only struggling but also feeling abandoned by God. And yet, instead of withdrawing, David poured out his heart to God. He was honest about what he was feeling. He may have been tired of trying, but he knew that God's love for him did not change because he was honest about what he was going through. David didn't shame himself, as we sometimes do, for feeling stuck or for wanting to give up. He simply acknowledged the truth, which was that his soul was exhausted.

Like David, you may be strong, but you're also a human being. That means you've probably been both full of faith and full of what-ifs and what-nows. You've prayed and worshiped with your whole heart, and you've had times when you couldn't even bring yourself to open your Bible. You've scaled mountains, and you've crawled on hands and knees just to make it through another day.

The Lord sees, the Lord knows, the Lord cares, and you can bring your honest cries to Him.

The Lord sees, the Lord knows, the Lord cares, and you can bring your honest cries to Him. His plans for you haven't changed, and His truth has not been revoked. You are still blessed, still set apart and called to good works in His Kingdom, regardless of what you're going through or how you feel. The Lord is not irritated with your exhaustion. On the contrary, He welcomes your little—your little strength, your little trust, your little plans, and your little faith.

Part of what I love about David's prayers is how he gives himself permission to put his entire self before God. He doesn't sugarcoat how he truly feels or deny the harsh reality of what he's facing. And yet, his honesty with God doesn't alienate him from God. Instead, it helps David to remember how much God loves him and how God has always been faithful and good. First, he prays with honesty, laying

HONESTY	AFFIRMATION
"Give ear to my words, O LORD; consider my groaning" (Psalm 5:1).	"But let all who take refuge in you rejoice; let them ever sing for joy, and spread your protection over them, that those who love your name may exult in you. For you bless the righteous, O LORD; you cover him with favor as with a shield" (Psalm 5:11-12).
"Be gracious to me, O LORD, for I am languishing; heal me, O LORD, for my bones are troubled. My soul also is greatly troubled. But you, O LORD— how long? . . . I am weary with my moaning; every night I flood my bed with tears; I drench my couch with my weeping. My eye wastes away because of grief; it grows weak because of all my foes" (Psalm 6:2-3, 6-7).	"The LORD has heard my plea; the LORD accepts my prayer. All my enemies shall be ashamed and greatly troubled; they shall turn back and be put to shame in a moment" (Psalm 6:9-10).
"Why, O LORD, do you stand far away? Why do you hide yourself in times of trouble?" (Psalm 10:1)	"O LORD, you hear the desire of the afflicted; you will strengthen their heart; you will incline your ear" (Psalm 10:17).
"How long, O LORD? Will you forget me forever? How long will you hide your face from me?" (Psalm 13:1).	"But I have trusted in your steadfast love; my heart shall rejoice in your salvation. I will sing to the LORD, because he has dealt bountifully with me" (Psalm 13:5-6).
"Turn to me and be gracious to me, for I am lonely and afflicted. The troubles of my heart are enlarged; bring me out of my distresses. Consider my affliction and my trouble, and forgive all my sins" (Psalm 25:16-18).	"Oh, guard my soul, and deliver me! Let me not be put to shame, for I take refuge in you. May integrity and uprightness preserve me, for I wait for you" (Psalm 25:20-21).

bare his feelings before God. Then he prays with affirmation as he remembers the goodness of God. Note how he does this for each of the example prayers by reading through the chart on page 153.

There are two things we can learn from David's prayers: It is important to be both honest about where we are and how we are feeling and just as important to turn our hearts back to truth and to who we know God to be, despite how we feel. Without the first, we are denying where we are, but without the other, we are denying what God can do. It might seem simple and inconsequential, but both are needed. When we declare where we are honestly, we are trusting God to love us where we're at, and yet we are also surrendering ourselves in the next breath to His sovereignty and trusting that His ways are always best for us, even when we have yet to understand. This is the basis for trust and intimacy we need with our good and loving heavenly Father.

REGAIN TRUST BY REFRAMING AND REBUILDING

We say all the time that being a Christian is not about a religion but about a relationship, and yet, we don't always make a connection between what a true relationship looks and feels like and our relationship with God. We say God loves us, and yet it feels selfish or prideful to consider what, specifically, God might love about us—how God might love us uniquely. We say God isn't a distant God, but we sometimes treat Him as if He is, especially if we withdraw when we're struggling. The trust God wants to build with us is built on the foundation of allowing Him to love us first, to give us the love we are so desperately craving.

We all want to be loved unconditionally. We want to know that even when we mess up, even when we struggle, we are still worth loving. We may believe intellectually that "God shows his love for us in that while we were still sinners, Christ died for us" (Romans 5:8), and yet, deep down, we still wonder if our struggles have disqualified us from love. Far from it, friend. When we come to faith in Jesus Christ, God sees us through the blood and sacrifice of Jesus. He chooses us and loves us, flaws and all. "I've seen it all," He says. "And I'm staying." Can we receive this from Him?

If these ideas of receiving from God and rebuilding trust with God are new to you, you might be asking the same question I asked of my counselor: *How?* While there are no magic formulas, there are some practical ways to rebuild trust with God, if we are willing. One that I've found especially helpful is to reframe and rebuild.

To *reframe* is to notice how we are looking at our current circumstances or relationships and then choose to see them differently. For example, if we have been framing life through the lenses of disappointment, bitterness, or frustration, we challenge those thoughts by changing our perspective. Perhaps the simplest example of reframing is whether we see the proverbial glass as half empty or half full. The amount of water in the glass remains the same; what changes is how we frame what we see.

To *rebuild* is to reconstruct our thinking based on the truth of God's Word. When something has been torn down and needs to be built again, it doesn't happen in a moment but rather one step at a time. And every new structure starts with a solid foundation. God's Word is the only foundation that will stand the test of time, and this is what we use to rebuild our thinking.

Together, reframing and rebuilding help us recognize where we have been so we can move forward with a new perspective. Jacob did some reframing and rebuilding immediately following his wrestle: "Jacob called the name of the place Peniel, saying, 'For I have seen God face to face, and yet my life has been delivered'" (Genesis 32:30).

Peniel means "face of God." Jacob could have chosen to define the place of his wrestle by what he suffered or by the wound he received. Instead, he reframed his wrestle by choosing to focus on the blessings of his encounter with God. And we can do the same.

I am still working on reframing and rebuilding my wrestle. It started in those early days as I sat with Sarah and considered the possibility that maybe God wasn't interested only in what I could do for Him but also in who I was to Him. That was my reframe—challenging my belief that God loved me only when I was productive. But I also had to rebuild by declaring and daring to believe the truth of His Word that says, "I have loved you with an everlasting love; therefore I have continued my faithfulness to you" (Jeremiah 31:3).

As you consider what reframing and rebuilding might mean for you, here are some additional reframing and rebuilding truths that have helped me on my own journey.

Reframe by receiving the truth that God understands. He understands your feelings, your hesitations, your difficult circumstances, and your pain. He is not in a hurry for you to "get over it," because He wants to walk with you in it (1 Peter 5:10).

Rebuild by choosing to accept His grace and love. When you become aware of the harsh things you say to yourself about how this process needs to happen faster or how you don't have enough faith, stop those thoughts in their tracks. Replace them with biblical truth. For example, "God gives me both encouragement and endurance to continue on in this" (see Romans 15:5).

Reframe by receiving the truth that you must confess mistrust. Trust can only be reestablished by confessing that you've lost it. Be honest with God about what happened that caused you to lose trust in Him. Remember, He already knows anyway (1 John 1:9).

Rebuild by choosing to ask God for help to trust again. It doesn't have to be a long prayer, it doesn't have to be full of impressive words, but the act of asking for God's mercy and grace will enable you to do that which you think you cannot (Matthew 21:22).

Reframe by receiving the truth that God has been present all along. He has been with you and loving you every step of the way, whether or not you were aware of it. God's Word tells us He will *never* leave us or forsake us (Hebrews 13:5).

Rebuild by choosing to recognize all the times God has ministered to you and worked for your healing. Go on a blessing hunt by making a list of every time God has come through for you or been faithful to you. Sometimes we don't see blessings because we aren't looking for them. Part of rebuilding trust is choosing to recognize all the ways God has been faithful to His promises (Numbers 23:19).

Reframe by receiving the truth that the places you are struggling are the places in which God intends to set you free. He wants to meet you in your struggles so that He can dig up the roots of whatever it is that continues to hurt you and so that you can be made new. His intentions are always for your good. He wants to set you free so you can become who He made you to be and receive all He has for you (John 8:32).

Rebuild by choosing to focus on who God is and that He will be faithful. We do this by allowing His Word to continue to renew our minds, bringing to mind how He has been faithful throughout Scripture, and listening to praise music to remind us how big our God is and all He is capable of (Philippians 1:6).

Friend, let God love you as you are and not how you think you should be. Reframing and rebuilding is not always easy work, but it is essential. The steps we take after the wrestle matter just as much as the wrestle itself because it's how we rebuild trust with God and move forward into the new life and new identity He has for us.

> **Friend, let God love you as you are and not how you think you should be.**

I believe you are already a warrior, a perseverer, and someone who is determined to hold on to God for the blessing that awaits on the other side of mistrust and your wrestle. This means you are already trying again. So why not surrender fully and receive the love God wants to lavish on you? Dare to believe that He loves you as you are, and that He *will* get you to where He wants you to be as you trust Him, one step at a time. And that is exactly what reframing and rebuilding look like, stepping forward in faith one choice at time.

STEP FORWARD IN FAITH

Having wrestled with God and received the blessing of his new name and new identity, Jacob, now Israel, was about to face his greatest fear. Would he trust God, or would he run away as he had in the past? Jacob had already prayed with honesty and affirmation:

> Please deliver me from the hand of my brother, from the hand of Esau, for I fear him, that he may come and attack me, the mothers with the children. But you said, "I will surely do you good, and make your offspring as the sand of the sea, which cannot be numbered for multitude."
> GENESIS 32:11-12

God's answer to Jacob's prayer was a wrestle that changed him, but now he had to take a step of faith and walk out his new identity in real life. Here's what happened when the sun rose after his night of wrestling:

> Jacob lifted up his eyes and looked, and behold, Esau was coming, and four hundred men with him. . . . [Jacob] himself went on before them, bowing himself to the ground seven times, until he came near to his brother. But Esau ran to meet him and embraced him and fell on his neck and kissed him, and they wept.
>
> GENESIS 33:1, 3-4

When Jacob was willing to face his brother despite his fears, God performed a miracle of reconciliation. Esau not only received Jacob but ran to meet him. Remember, Jacob had expected rejection at best and the slaughter of his entire family at worst. Instead, Esau embraced him and wept at being reunited with his long-lost brother. All this happened because Jacob dared to step forward in faith after his wrestle.

It's a beautiful picture of how love works, isn't it? Love runs to be reunited with the beloved. That's how I imagine God responding to us when we decide to trust Him and take a step of faith. While we anticipate being met with disappointment and rejection, God rushes to embrace us right where we are. No one is more excited about our trust and restored relationship than He is!

If stepping forward in faith required Jacob to face a brother who had previously wanted him dead, what might it require of you? After you have made the choice to reframe and rebuild trust, how do you move forward in faith? Here are some ideas to get you started.

Remind yourself of all God continues to call you to. Wrestling seasons have a point, but they aren't the point. God still has a lifelong journey for you to take, other lives He wants you to touch, relationships He wants to restore, and a message He wants to release through you. Moving on means trusting that your story and His purposes for you are still unfolding and taking the risk to find out what those purposes are by stepping forward in faith.

Face your "what-ifs" head on. God has met you in this wrestle to bring you clarity about both who He is and who you are in Him. While you don't know how facing your what-ifs will turn out or if more pain will meet you, moving forward in faith means you choose to trust God and let go of the outcomes.

Equip yourself with practical tools. Moving forward will be its own kind of struggle, but you don't have to enter into it unprepared. Knowing that the enemy will tempt you with doubt, exhaustion, or distractions, you can prepare for those things by identifying a strategy ahead of time.

- When you don't have time to read your Bible, listen to an audio Bible while you commute or do chores around the house.
- When you feel discouraged, listen to an empowering sermon.
- When you feel anxious, avoid overstimulating yourself on social media.
- When you feel overwhelmed, take out a pad of paper or the notes app on your phone and make two lists—one of the absolute necessities and another of the things that can wait.
- When you can't seem to catch a break or your faith feels weak, listen to worship music and declare the truth of those words over your life and circumstances.

- When you feel lonely, be the one to reach out by texting a friend something you love about them.
- When you feel like you don't have enough, look around you and make a mental list of all the things you have been given that are in that space.

Stepping forward in faith often feels scary, but if we take these steps knowing that frustration or discouragement may come from time to time, we will know how to respond when they do. It's only human to want guarantees that the risks we take will all work out, but that is just not how faith works. When Jacob's wrestle was over, he had to move toward his fear without knowing what might happen when he did, and we will often have to do the same.

FEELING SAFE WHEN VULNERABLE

Why be intentional about moving on by reframing our thoughts and rebuilding our trust with God? Because if we don't, we will never walk by faith. We might want to think we can coddle our fears and walk by faith, but it is not possible. We will cling to either one or the other. To really trust God means that we feel safe entrusting Him with every aspect of our lives: our strengths, our gifts, and our opportunities, but also our failings, our doubts, and our exhaustion. All these things make up who we are. We are never going to always be strong, that is why we need Jesus so desperately.

God has always done things the only way He knows how—perfectly and with great love. Somewhere along the way, our pain made us doubt this could be true, but despite our feelings, it didn't cease to be true. Choosing to trust the Lord again means placing everything we are at His feet and believing

Trusting God is always worth the risk—always.

Him when He says, "I've seen it all, and I'm staying." This is unconditional love.

God has always been worth trusting. Even when He has said no, and we have wrestled with the pain of our unanswered questions, He was still loving us best. It's important to be honest with God about our struggles, but it's also important to move on when we're ready. To stay where we are indefinitely is to give up, and that is not who we are. Trusting God is always worth the risk—always.

10

BLESSED TO BE CHANGED

God will not permit any troubles
to come upon us, unless He has a
specific plan by which great blessing
can come out of the difficulty.
PETER MARSHALL,
A Man Called Peter

PERHAPS YOU'VE HEARD THE SAYING, "Don't live the same year
seventy-five times and call it a life." As hard and painful as change
and wrestling seasons might be, when we look back on our lives,
we want to be able to see that we are no longer the same person we
once were. The Lord knows that if we are never challenged, we will
never change. And if we never change, we will remain stuck in self-
defeating patterns of belief and behavior we were never meant to be
stuck in. As familiar as they may be, those stuck places are prisons.
That is why God invites us to wrestle—not to punish us, but to set
us free and to push us into becoming who He created us to be.

My wrestling season was marked deeply by anxiety and depression, but I knew I didn't want to stay in that place and that I could
not stay there. No matter how painful the process was, I wanted to

hold on to God with everything I had because I chose to believe what He said was possible, even if I hadn't seen it yet. The Lord began to show me how to renew my mind, one thought at a time. I began to see that an unchecked mind was the path to an exhausted internal life. If I am honest, this is a process I continue to trust the Lord with to this day. My negative and hurtful thought patterns had been so ingrained that I didn't even realize it was my thoughts themselves that were hurting me. But as I started to pay attention to what I was thinking, God taught me how to intentionally break those patterns and change began to occur.

> **The blessing of change is the ability to see that we can think differently, believe differently, and respond differently.**

The blessing of change is the ability to see that we can think differently, believe differently, and respond differently. Maybe in our ideal world, we would prefer that the Lord rescue us completely out of what we are facing, but what He often does instead is show us the power and blessing of depending on Him to get through it.

The apostle Paul acknowledged the relationship between his own weaknesses and God's strength in his second letter to the church at Corinth:

> So to keep me from becoming conceited because of the surpassing greatness of the revelations, a thorn was given me in the flesh, a messenger of Satan to harass me, to keep me from becoming conceited. Three times I pleaded with the Lord about this, that it should leave me. But he said to me, "My grace is sufficient for you, for my power is made perfect in weakness." Therefore I will boast all the more gladly of my weaknesses, so that the power of Christ may rest upon me. For the sake of

Christ, then, I am content with weaknesses, insults, hardships, persecutions, and calamities. For when I am weak, then I am strong.

2 CORINTHIANS 12:7-10

God wants us to change and move forward, but not in our own strength. We were never meant to do life without Him, and we need His strength, truth, and peace as we continue to tackle our difficulties head-on. Our weaknesses remain not because God lacks compassion, but to keep us intimately connected to Him. God knows we cannot become who He wants us to become or accomplish the kingdom work He has given us to do without relying on His strength.

SAME STRUGGLE, NEW STRATEGY

So how do we address self-defeating beliefs and patterns, especially the negative and hurtful thoughts that keep us trapped? It's one thing to quote Romans 12:2 (NIV), "Be transformed by the renewing of your mind," and another thing altogether to do it. How do we, in fact, "take every thought captive" (2 Corinthians 10:5)? How does the average girl trying to get through her average day do that? By identifying new strategies to address the same struggles.

For this average girl, taking my thoughts captive started by simply noticing them. For example, when I went to church, I noticed that my mind would immediately begin to tell me a story of why so-and-so was ignoring me or giving me weird looks. In response to that story, I noticed that I began feeling defensive and insecure, and then I would withdraw or have a completely made-up argument with said person in my mind. That's when I realized, *Oh! This is an all-hands-on-deck moment—these thoughts are getting wild in here. Emergency action required!* Then I would immediately try to interrupt those thoughts in any way I could.

My go-to strategy was the one I talked about in chapter 5, which was saying out loud, "I love you." When I used that phrase, it was as if the voice of God was interrupting my downward spiral of lies with truth: "Even if all that stuff you're making up in your head is true, which is unlikely, I *still* love you." So, as I stood there in church with my thoughts taking me down a path I didn't want to be on, I would blurt out, "I love you." And as weird as it might have seemed to anyone who happened to walk by and hear me say it to myself, let me tell you, it worked.

I also had to come up with a new strategy for pressures, insecurities, and frustrations I was battling as a people pleaser. For years, I felt crushed when people weren't happy with me. I took on responsibility for their happiness, not considering that maybe they just weren't happy with themselves. I thought, *Maybe I can make them happy with me by trying harder. If I were a better Christian and could respond in a more calm and loving way, maybe I wouldn't feel so bad.* Once I started noticing my thoughts, alarm bells immediately began ringing when I began to think this way. *Wait! Aren't these the same exact thoughts that landed me in a deep pit and left me tired of trying to begin with? Aren't these the same thoughts the Lord and I had been wrestling over? What should I do now instead?*

The truth was, I not only didn't know how to change, I was also afraid that I couldn't. But once again, little by little, the Lord began to reveal to me that I had freely received the grace I needed for salvation, and I could also freely receive the grace I needed for transformation. I had somehow come to believe that change was completely up to me. This, my friend, had led to my exhaustion because it just was not possible for me to change in my own strength. God began to reveal to me that I needed to rely on His grace to change me. My part was simply to acknowledge I needed help, ask Him for it, and then wait for Him to help me. When the next step became clear, I needed to be willing to say, "Okay, Lord, if you say so. I'll do it."

Walking in change by faith requires vulnerable dependence. When I tried to fix myself or make myself feel better, I remained in control. But to give up trying all my own ways and trust God? That was scary. And the Lord wasn't short on giving me opportunities to practice.

There was one relationship that was especially difficult for me. I felt gripped by overwhelming anxiety and fear when this family member was angry at me over things I could not control or over boundaries I had set. I felt the panic start in my chest and then rush to my head. *What is my strategy now, Lord? Because I'm in freak-out mode!* Fortunately, He had one for me.

God helped me to see that the enemy wanted to exploit this weakness in me. He wanted me to live in panic mode, hoping I would question God's goodness, doubt the change He had made in my life, and distrust God and turn my back on Him again. But I realized that I didn't have to follow the enemy's script. If his intent was to turn me away from God, what if I did the exact opposite instead? What if, instead of letting the weight of being misunderstood and disliked crush me, I chose to turn toward the Lord and worship Him? What if I declared His greatness, His majesty, His faithfulness, His goodness? That would be the exact opposite of what the enemy wanted. So I decided that worship would be my strategy for hitting back.

My struggle remained the same, but because of what I had been through, my strategy changed. Every time there was flare-up with this family member, I literally ran to put on my headphones so I could listen to music that helped me worship the Lord.

Not. Today. Satan.

After singing about God's goodness and faithfulness, I could feel the strength of the Lord sustaining me. This was certainly not the response the enemy wanted, and it was what God used to help me experience the blessing of change, one small choice of trust at a time.

The way we have always struggled may persist even as we begin walking in our new identities, but we can learn to respond in a new way—and it works!

The way we have always struggled may persist even as we begin walking in our new identities, but we can learn to respond in a new way—and it works!

Jacob was no different. Although his wrestle with God had ended, the drama of life did not. Between Genesis 32 and 35, Jacob faced many more hardships and tests of his faith. He must have been full of stress and dread. At this time, he had already been renamed and blessed by God, but there was no happily-ever-after ending, because real life isn't like the fairy tales. Receiving the blessing of the wrestle isn't a "get out of trials free card," but rather a Spirit-empowered ability to see trials and move through them differently.

Jacob found himself in desperate need. And yet, when he was in a place of fear, he responded much differently—as one who knew the power of the God with whom he had wrestled.

So Jacob said to his household and to all who were with him, "Put away the foreign gods that are among you and purify yourselves and change your garments. Then let us arise and go up to Bethel, so that I may make there an altar to the God who answers me in the day of my distress and has been with me wherever I have gone."
GENESIS 35:2-3

This time, Jacob trusted in the ability of his God to deliver him and knew what needed to be done. He told his family to set aside false gods and to seek the Lord, their only true source of strength and protection. Jacob had the same struggles, but he also had a whole new strategy that enabled him to deal with them in God's strength.

THE BLESSING OF GOD

God did not disappoint Jacob. In fact, He reiterated Jacob's new name, confirmed the change that He had brought in Jacob's life, and promised him even more blessings to come.

> God appeared to Jacob again, when he came from Paddan-aram, and blessed him. And God said to him, "Your name is Jacob; no longer shall your name be called Jacob, but Israel shall be your name." So he called his name Israel. And God said to him, "I am God Almighty: be fruitful and multiply. A nation and a company of nations shall come from you, and kings shall come from your own body. The land that I gave to Abraham and Isaac I will give to you, and I will give the land to your offspring after you."
> GENESIS 35:9-12

Why did God reiterate Jacob's name change? Some scholars believe that because the Genesis 32 passage describes Jacob's opponent as a man, this encounter makes it clear that Jacob was being addressed by God Himself, El Shaddai, who was now confirming both the name change and the blessing, and even adding to the blessing.

God commanded Jacob to be fruitful and multiply and confirmed that nations and kings would be among his descendants. The Lord also assured him of provision, promising that He would give Jacob the land that had been promised and given to his father and grandfather.

And this, my friend, is another thing I love about God. When God does something in our lives, when He bestows a blessing, it cannot be revoked. God is not wishy-washy and uncertain in what He wants to do. What He says, stands. We might struggle, we might act like our old selves, we might fall down and have to get back up, and we most definitely will need to continue to run back to Him for strength and guidance again and again, but this we must never forget—that He is the faithful one.

God's Word is full of examples of His faithfulness to His people. He knows our weaknesses, our failings, the way we waver and forget. He isn't looking for us to be perfect. What He is looking for is people who will continue to get up when we fall and walk by faith anyway. Will we be people who stand on who He is and what He does? Will we choose to remember what He has brought us through and how He has changed us?

If there ever comes a time when you doubt what God has done in you, when you begin to resent that you ever had to wrestle, stand on God's Word. It never fails. Here are some verses you can declare over your life when you find yourself flailing or faltering.

> *I will not be shaken.* "I keep my eyes always on the LORD. With him at my right hand, I will not be shaken" (Psalm 16:8, NIV).
> *I am not condemned.* "There is therefore now no condemnation for those who are in Christ Jesus" (Romans 8:1).
> *I will be blessed when I am steadfast.* "Blessed is the man who remains steadfast under trial, for when he has stood the test he will receive the crown of life, which God has promised to those who love him" (James 1:12).

I do not have to fear. "For God gave us a spirit not of fear
  but of power and love and self-control" (2 Timothy 1:7).
I will see the goodness of God. "I remain confident of this:
  I will see the goodness of the LORD in the land of the living"
  (Psalm 27:13, NIV).
God will be my strength. "On the day I called, you
  answered me; my strength of soul you increased"
  (Psalm 138:3).
I do not have to fear others' opinions. "The fear of man
  lays a snare, but whoever trusts in the LORD is safe"
  (Proverbs 29:25).

Write these down on cards or sticky notes and post them where
you will see them throughout the day. These statements capture the
truth of who you are, who God is, and what He will do for you when
you feel weak or doubt your place with Him. Use God's Word and
worship to continue moving forward in what He is doing in you so
that He can continue to work through you.

EMBRACING BEING MADE NEW

We really can make new choices that enable us, over time, to walk
in the blessing of change. We can increasingly experience more of
God's perfect power, peace, and presence. We can be sure that God
will do what He says He will do. But even as we begin to experience
these blessings, we need to remember that when God changes us, the
change is both immediate and a process. That's how it was not only
for Jacob, but for others in the Bible as well.

In the New Testament, one of the most compelling examples
of change that is both immediate and a process is Jesus changing
Simon's name to Peter:

> [Jesus] said to them, "But who do you say that I am?" Simon
> Peter replied, "You are the Christ, the Son of the living God."
> And Jesus answered him, "Blessed are you, Simon Bar-Jonah!
> For flesh and blood has not revealed this to you, but my Father
> who is in heaven. And I tell you, you are Peter, and on this rock
> I will build my church, and the gates of hell shall not prevail
> against it."
>
> MATTHEW 16:15-18

It's interesting to note that even after Jesus gave him a new name, he was still often referred to as Simon or even with both names, Simon Peter.

I would like to suggest that on this side of heaven, our process of sanctification—of becoming more like Christ—includes walking in who we have always been as well as in who we are becoming.

I love Peter, as many people do. I think it's because he is so relatable. He was full of good intentions and passion that often got him into trouble. I love him because I can be the exact same way, and one day it struck me that the Lord knew exactly what He was getting when He chose Peter to be His disciple and ultimately appointed him to build the early church—and He chose Peter anyway.

The same is true for you and me. The Lord knows who we are from the start. He has been working with and using flawed and messed-up people from the beginning of time. If He had to wait for us to get ourselves together, He knows better than anyone that He would be waiting a long time.

I believe what the Lord loved about Peter was his heart. It was clear that Peter had a lot to learn and a lot to go through, but Jesus knew Peter wouldn't give up because of his failings or shortcomings.

He wasn't perfect, but he was wildly committed to Jesus, to learning and growing, to getting up and starting over when he fell.

Jesus affirmed this about Peter even when He knew Peter was about to deny Him. In an intimate conversation, Jesus both acknowledged what Peter would have to endure and encouraged him. Note how He referred to him as both Simon and as Peter.

> "Simon, Simon, behold, Satan demanded to have you, that he might sift you like wheat, but I have prayed for you that your faith may not fail. And when you have turned again, strengthen your brothers." Peter said to him, "Lord, I am ready to go with you both to prison and to death." Jesus said, "I tell you, Peter, the rooster will not crow this day, until you deny three times that you know me."
>
> LUKE 22:31-34

Even after walking closely with Jesus for three years, after hearing all His teachings and being instructed by Him personally, Peter was still reliant on his own strength. He was certain of his own loyalty, and his pride prompted him to make declarations Jesus knew he was not yet able to live up to.

Satan had asked to sift Peter as wheat. When wheat was sifted, it was shaken violently or sometimes thrown to the ground to separate the grain from the chaff so that the wind could blow the chaff away. It was not going to be an easy process, and Satan no doubt had the intention of destroying his faith so his doubts would cause him to walk away from Jesus. But we know that God can always use for good what Satan intends for evil (Genesis 50:20).

But Jesus also said something remarkable to Peter: "I have prayed for you that your faith may not fail." Jesus knew that Peter was about to betray Him. In all their time together, Jesus had seen how dependent Peter was on his own strength and how proud he was of it. Jesus knew Peter's faith would be shaken when he experienced the great shame of denying the one he had vowed he would never abandon. So before any of that happened, Jesus told Peter, "I have prayed for you that your faith may not fail."

There will be times when we, like Peter, might become overconfident in what we have learned from God to the point that we slide from depending on God to depending on what we have learned about God. But God will be faithful to us, anticipating that we will fall, but also interceding for us (Romans 8:26), as Jesus did for Peter, so that our faith will not fail.

The same grace we learned to lean on in our wrestle is the grace we need to rely on as we learn to continue walking, always increasingly dependent on our God. And when we stray, get off track, or realize we aren't walking in the way the Lord has called us to walk, we can pray, "Lord, I see how I need to change, but I don't know how to do it. You are the faithful one. Help me to rely on your strength as I become who you have called me to be."

And let's not forget the last part of Jesus' statement to Peter: "And *when* you have turned again, strengthen your brothers" (Luke 22:32, emphasis added). What a beautiful encouragement and commission! Even though He knew Peter would fail, Jesus assured Peter that his return wasn't a matter of *if* but *when*. Because Jesus had full confidence that Peter would return, He put Peter in charge of encouraging the other disciples.

Look at your watch or your phone and jot down the time. Taking a moment to write it down will make this moment, the moment you put your pen to paper, a marked moment. From now going forward, whenever you need to check the time, allow it to be a reminder of two things: Time brings change, and change takes time. God is not as impatient with us as we are with ourselves. He is the faithful one.

Not us, but Him.

Not our strength, but His.

Not to us, but to Him be the glory.

We commit to learning how to be dependent on God after coming through a wrestle with the Lord because we have the same assignment Jesus gave to Peter—to strengthen our brothers and sisters.

WALKING WITH A LIMP

When God engages us in a wrestling season, it is not to change our circumstances but to teach us how to deal with each new battle and struggle as we move forward with a new perspective. Our blessing is having been changed from the inside out. So, just as God did with Jacob, He allows us to walk with a limp.

After Jacob had wrestled and received the blessing of God, he moved on, but not without a bodily reminder of how dependent he was on God. "So Jacob called the name of the place Peniel, saying, 'For I have seen God face to face, and yet my life has been delivered.' The sun rose upon him as he passed Penuel, limping because of his hip" (Genesis 32:30-31).

The sun rose on Jacob's life again, and yet he also remained marked by his experience because his hip had been injured in the process. Jacob walked away from his wrestle with a limp, and many believe that he lived with that limp until the day he died, a constant reminder of what he had been through and who he had become.

The wrestle changes us, and we will be forever marked by what we've been through—which means we'll need to learn to navigate life differently.

So what does it mean to walk with a limp? It means, in part, that the limp you now bear is both a mark of victory and a mark of weakness you may carry throughout your life. It's not a sinful weakness, but rather a weakness that continually points you to your need to rely on God. Your limp is a mark of your relationship with God and the blessing of transformation He has released in you through your wrestle.

If your wrestle has been grief, your limp may be that you are known as someone who has suffered a great loss of some kind and learned how to navigate the unknown path that was forced upon you. Walking with your limp requires that you rely on God's comfort and strength, and it also makes you easy to identify as someone who can offer support and compassion to others who are grieving. Your new way of moving through life is now as one who knows the deep pain of loss and can minister in powerful ways to those who are entering those treacherous waters themselves. At first, it may feel painful and awkward that people see you in this way, but you will eventually begin to see that it is also a blessing because of the overflow of compassion you now have to give to others.

If your wrestle has been with a chronic health condition, your limp serves as a constant reminder of how you need God's strength, and it also marks you as one whom God has gifted to minister to others. People who are struggling with health issues recognize you as someone they can trust and turn to for wisdom and advice because you have walked the path they are on. Your pain is your marker, but it is also a supernatural grace and gift that God uses to help others.

If your wrestle has been with a broken relationship, your limp makes you constantly aware of how you need God's strength and wisdom, and it marks you as someone who knows how to lean on God through a long and painful struggle. You have been forever changed in the grace you give to yourself and to others. Your limp has given you wisdom and credibility to point others to the promise that in all things, God really can and will work for the good of those who love Him (Romans 8:28).

You likely never wanted to walk with a limp, but you have one anyway. No one gets through this life pain-free, and it's what we choose to do with our pain that matters most. Our limps mark what we have learned and who we are becoming. No one can speak with as much authority and compassion as someone who has done the hard work of wrestling with God. Your limp both anchors you in God's strength and gives you a story to share with a world that is desperate for hope.

> No one gets through this life pain-free, and it's what we choose to do with our pain that matters most.

Only those who dare to wrestle with God are marked in such obvious ways, forever changed, just as Jacob was. Your wrestle and the choice you make to hang on to God through it all means that now, with every forward step, your life will be marked by the experience you have come through. That includes the way you think, the way you make decisions, the way you interact with God, the grace you give yourself when you fail, and the way you offer compassion, grace, and guidance to others because of what you have been through. Every step we take is a reminder of who we used to be, the encounter we had with the living God who loves us, and who He is helping us to become.

Learning to walk with a limp might feel uncomfortable and awkward at first. There will likely be a learning curve, and it will take some practice to find your new rhythm. There might be times when you are tempted to go back to your old ways of thinking and doubting, looking for comfort in your disappointment or indulging bitterness that you ever had to wrestle at all. But let your limp—your weaknesses—always remind you that this is no longer an option. Remember what you have been through and how it has forever changed you. Be patient with yourself. Learning a new way to walk through life—to allow for your weaknesses—may make you uncomfortable for a while, but soon it will feel like second nature.

Every day we get to practice. We can acknowledge our limps, notice our thoughts, and implement our new strategies. These places in our lives that have been marked by struggle may look like weaknesses, but they are actually the places where God has blessed us with the gift of life change.

BLESSED TO BE A BLESSING

There is no more effective healer than
a wounded healer, and in the process the
wounded healer's own scars may fade away.
PHILIP YANCEY,
Where Is God When It Hurts?

WHEN JACOB FEARED FOR HIS LIFE before facing his brother, Esau, he could never have known that God would soon give him a new identity and a new name, Israel. He could never have guessed that God's promised blessing would include nations and kings in his lineage or that thousands of years later, the Jewish nation would still be called by the name Israel. And yet, his willingness to accept God's invitation to the wrestle and to walk with God in the years that followed has left a legacy of faith for God's people to this very day.

The writer of Hebrews includes Jacob in the well-known "Hall of Faith," saying, "By faith Jacob, when he was dying, blessed each of Joseph's sons, and worshiped as he leaned on the top of his staff" (Hebrews 11:21, NIV). Scholars believe the mention of him leaning on his staff is an acknowledgment that he still needed support for the limp he received while wrestling with God. What a wonderful picture this verse gives us of Jacob—as he is leaning on his staff, he is also passing on the blessing given to him amid his pain and struggle. That blessing wasn't for him alone but for his children, his grandchildren, and the entire nation of Israel for generations to come.

What if Jacob had refused the wrestle? What if he had run away? What if he had given up and refused to hang on? What if he hadn't allowed himself to be changed through that long and painful night? We don't know for certain, but I doubt Jacob would have been included in the list of Faith Hall of Famers in Hebrews 11.

We may not be physical descendants of the Hebrew patriarchs, but we are spiritual descendants, and our decision to follow God—to accept the invitation to wrestle—has the potential to leave the same kind of faith legacy that Jacob's decision to wrestle did. We may not be able to imagine now how our legacy will play out, but our choice to wrestle will undoubtedly impact the lives of those around us.

The choices we make to engage God in the hardest parts of our lives matter—they matter for today, and they matter for the future. Our lives are living parables that people are watching and learning from. Those who don't know God are watching to see the difference faith makes when we face the same kind of hardships they do.

What choice will we make? Will we accept God's invitation to the wrestle? When we are living with an ache and feel overcome with "whys," will we choose to trust God one day at a time as He wipes one tear at a time from our faces? Will we choose to hold on to God until we make it to the other side of our wrestle, or will we choose not to? Will we obey God? Will we trust God? Will we believe God, even in this? All of these choices are real, and all of them have the potential to diminish or multiply God's blessing for generations to come.

WILL WE BELIEVE GOD FOR HIS BLESSING?

Every time I read the story of the Israelites—the same Israelites named after our wrestler—wandering in the desert for those forty years, it makes me a little sad. Maybe it makes me sad because I see myself in them, especially my proclivity to mistrust God when the journey feels too long and too uncomfortable. I can almost hear my soul nodding in frustrated agreement, *Yes, I want to be free, but not like this. This is too hard.*

Time after time, the Lord asked the wandering Israelites to trust Him and promised that He had blessings for them if they would just believe Him and push on. Their victory was guaranteed, but it was a victory they could not yet see or comprehend. All they could see was their pain and suffering. Instead of following God, they followed their fears and, ultimately, a whole generation died in the wilderness because of their unbelief.

> Caleb quieted the people before Moses and said, "Let us go up at once and occupy it, for we are well able to overcome it." Then the men who had gone up with him said, "We are not able to go up against the people, for they are stronger than we are." So they brought to the people of Israel a bad report of the land that they had spied out.
> NUMBERS 13:30-32

Here is how the writer of Hebrews describes those who chose not to trust God's promise:

> As it is said,
>> "Today, if you hear his voice,
>> do not harden your hearts as in the rebellion."

> For who were those who heard and yet rebelled? Was it
> not all those who left Egypt led by Moses? And with whom was
> he provoked for forty years? Was it not with those who sinned,
> whose bodies fell in the wilderness? And to whom did he
> swear that they would not enter his rest, but to those who were
> disobedient? So we see that they were unable to enter because
> of unbelief.
>
> **HEBREWS 3:15-19**

While most of them died there in the wilderness, there were two, Joshua and Caleb, who dared to take God at His word and to act in faith. May we, too, dare to believe God, no matter the difficulties that lie before us. When our paths look hard or even impossible, let us follow the lead of Joshua and Caleb, who took God at His word. Let us choose to trust our God to do what He says He will do. With Jacob, let us hold on for dear life to the one who faces us in the wrestle.

> Let us choose to trust our God to do what He says He will do.

So how do we do this? We start simply by being faithful in the smallest of ways. We make the small daily choices that add up to a lifetime of walking by faith.

- We choose to set our minds on thoughts that align with His Word.
- We read and declare His Word over our lives and circumstances.
- We look for the places where God is moving and join Him there.
- We cry out continually for His grace to help us keep moving forward.

When we choose each day to love again, get back up again, believe God's Word again, and do what we sense He is asking of us, even if that is simply receiving His love, we are choosing to trust God. We are choosing to keep our hearts soft and open to the Blesser.

When we choose each day to love again, get back up again, believe God's Word again, and do what we sense He is asking of us, even if that is simply receiving His love, we are choosing to trust God.

Soon, we will begin to experience the blessing—our tiredness turns into boldness, our hopelessness becomes overflowing joy, and we know that the wrestle was worth it. We are not the same, and we never will be again.

TELL YOUR STORY

Your wrestle is a living story, one you can tell to build God's Kingdom and see His glory come! Just as He did with Jacob, God has entrusted you with a message, and He wants to release His power and goodness to others through you. When others receive their invitation to the wrestle, you can call out to them, "Keep holding on, God is faithful!" That is the testimony of everyone who wrestles and perseveres with God.

The last book of the Bible offers us a beautiful picture of just how powerful our stories are:

> And I heard a loud voice in heaven, saying, "Now the salvation and the power and the kingdom of our God and the authority of his Christ have come, for the accuser of our brothers has been thrown down, who accuses them day and night before our God. And they have conquered him by the blood of the Lamb and by the word of their testimony, for they loved not their lives even unto death."
> REVELATION 12:10-11

Did you catch how we overcome our enemy? By the blood of the Lamb and the *word of our testimony*. In other words, we defeat the enemy of our souls by receiving salvation and by telling others what the Lord has done in and through us. That's the kind of power our wrestling stories have.

The body of Christ needs your story. The psalmist proclaims, "Let the redeemed of the LORD tell their story—those he redeemed from the hand of the foe" (Psalm 107:2, NIV). Ask God for an opportunity to share what He has done for you. Write it down for your children or your grandchildren, share it in your small group, church, or with a friend over coffee. Declare the faithfulness of God through your wrestle with someone in your life who is also tired of trying. Every time you tell the story of how God has helped you overcome, you conquer the enemy and multiply God's blessing.

God calls all of us to face our own brokenness. We can't make disciples for His Kingdom until we become disciples ourselves, fully submitting ourselves to His teaching, training, correction, and humbling in our own lives. We can't lead others where we have never been. We know what God's love looks like because we have been desperate for it ourselves and have learned that the only way to be loved is to receive God's love, especially when we feel undeserving. When we learn what grace is and how to receive it from Him, we have grace to give away. Our wrestling story is now our testimony because we don't just know about God's blessing, we have lived it!

As I continued in my own journey, I knew I wanted to share what God had done in me. I often still cry when I remember the dark thoughts I once had and the hopelessness I used to feel in contrast to the joy I now experience every day. I feel overwhelming gratitude every time I think about how far the Lord has brought me. No one knows joy as profoundly as one who has wrestled with God through the dark of night and now lives the blessing of change that once seemed impossible.

The more I saw the change Jesus had made in my life, the more I wanted others to know this was possible for them as well. One of the first times I was able to share my story with a small group, a woman came up to me afterward and said she was in the same exact place I had been. She said she was feeling hopeless and lost, but that hearing my story gave her hope that God hadn't left her alone in her pain but was with her in it. *Wow.*

Every meetup with a friend for coffee, every prayer for a coworker with a broken heart, and every encouraging comment on social media became an opportunity to pass on hope, love, and the faith that God is still at work. Being loved by God in my darkest moments gave me a level of compassion I had not known before and a purpose to continue telling others how good He is, because I knew it firsthand.

WHY WE WRESTLE

When we're wrestling, believing in God's blessing is hard, and trusting God is hard, but so is living in defeat, doubt, and disappointment for the rest of our lives.

This is why we wrestle.

God does not force us to believe Him or walk by faith. It is a choice we make in each new season of our lives.

This is why we wrestle.

Our culture wants us to believe that this life is about trying to get the best and easiest life we can for ourselves and our families. But we know the truth—God is more concerned with who we are becoming than how comfortable we are.

This is why we wrestle.

We know that there are others who are about to step into the same fears, doubts, and pains we have just wrestled through. They are look-ing for hope that God is faithful and will get them to the other side.

This is why we wrestle.

Our children are watching. We want to leave a legacy of faith that says, no matter how bad it gets, the Lord is worth holding on to.

This is why we wrestle.

We are prone to depend on ourselves, to rely on our own strengths and our own understanding. Without reminders of how dependent we are on God, we begin to think God should submit to our idea of how it's all supposed to go down rather than the other way around.

This is why we wrestle.

When our surrender to the Lord requires laying aside every last bit of the things we are trying to hold on to so tightly, we discover what we really believe. Too often we discover that fear rather than Jesus has become our true master.

This is why we wrestle.

The Lord will never be satisfied with just part of our hearts; He came to take over. He invites us to wrestle and ultimately to surrender—to empty our hands so He can fill them with what we really need, which is more of Him.

This is why we wrestle.

In the wrestle and beyond, we declare over and over again, "I am not the King, and this is not my Kingdom. Your Kingdom come, Lord, and your will be done on earth as it is in heaven" (see Matthew 6:10).

And so may our hearts confess:

My rights, I lay them down.
My plans, I lay them down.
My gifts and talents, I lay them down.
My fears, I lay them down.

My disappointments, I lay them down.

My lack and all the things that hurt me, scare me, excite me, or intimidate me, I lay them down.

Greater is He than everything we lay down. He is the only worthy one! We live to serve one King and one Kingdom.

If God has you in a season of wrestling, I know you are in a hurry to get out. But know that the Lord is with you. He is doing a work in you that is far beyond anything you can imagine or comprehend.

Trust Him.

He is not in a rush, and He doesn't expect you to hurry up and fix yourself. He knows just how long your wrestle will take, and He wants you to learn to trust Him for every moment, to ask Him every question, and to realize that freedom comes when you bring your burden and lay it on Him. He wants to carry it for you, to take it from you, to give you joy in exchange for your grief. He promises that His yoke is easy, and His burden is light (Matthew 11:30). And there is so much blessing that can come through being broken.

My prayer for you is that the Holy Spirit would fill your heart and that you would be assured as you never have been before that the Lord cares for you and will never abandon you. I pray that as you press into the wrestle, you get to know

In the wrestle and beyond, we declare over and over again, "I am not the King, and this is not my Kingdom. Your Kingdom come, Lord, and your will be done on earth as it is in heaven."

God more intimately than you have ever known Him before. I pray that God brings you supernatural power to hold on to Him until you come to the other side transformed. I pray the Lord fills you with a hunger for His Word and a desire and willingness to obey, no matter what it costs. I pray God helps you receive His love and that you experience it in a way you cannot deny. I pray that you use your wrestle to light the world on fire with the truth of who God is and what He is capable of.

Not to us, Lord. But to you be the glory.

In Jesus' name, amen.

QUESTIONS FOR REFLECTION

INTRO

1. How are you feeling toward God right now, and what circumstances or struggles are affecting your relationship with Him?

2. What things do you sense God inviting you to wrestle over? What emotions do you feel when you think of entering the battle? What, if anything, frightens you about the prospect of wrestling with God?

3. Has there been a time in the past when God brought you through a season of wrestling? What changes did you experience because of that?

CHAPTER 1

1. What frustrations are you struggling with right now? What pain are you experiencing because of each frustration?

2. What misguided actions, if any, have you taken as a result of your frustration? What were the consequences of these actions?

3. How might reframing your frustration and pain have a purpose in your life?

CHAPTER 2

1. In what ways has God hurt your feelings or disappointed you? Spend some time journaling and sitting with your questions and doubts—God isn't turned away by them. In fact, He is waiting for you to be honest about your struggles and enter the wrestle.

2. How does it make you feel to know that Jesus wrestled too, and He still got a no from God the Father?

3. This chapter outlined three tools to help you hold on to faith in the midst of the wrestle: let yourself feel, recognize your progress, and surround yourself with support. What is your response to these tools? Do you agree these might help you as you wrestle? In what ways might you make use of them?

CHAPTER 3

1. Briefly recall the prayers you've prayed over the past week. On a scale of 1 to 10 (1 being completely *dishonest* and 10 being completely *honest*), how honest were your prayers? What, if anything, prevents you from being vulnerable with the God who already sees you and knows you better than you know yourself?

2. Why do you think God answered Jacob's prayer by wrestling with him?

3. What lies have you been believing about God? What might it mean for you to call them lies and take every thought captive to truth?

CHAPTER 4

1. What unrealistic and unspoken expectations might you be putting on yourself? On others? In what ways do these expectations make you feel tired of trying?

2. As you reflect on the stories of Gideon, the widow of Zarephath, and Elijah, which one do you most resonate with, and why? What do you sense God might be inviting you to be honest about?

3. What do the stories of Gideon, the widow of Zarephath, and Elijah reveal about God's character and His care for His people?

CHAPTER 5

1. What do you think it means that the man (God) wrestling with Jacob "saw that he did not prevail" (Genesis 32:25)? What principles does that seem to communicate?

2. What do you sense God may be doing in your life to move you from self-reliance to God-reliance?

3. What lies are you tempted to believe right now? List three lies you believe and practice speaking truth or thought pattern

interrupters over them. What do you hope might change if you lived like what God says about you is true?

CHAPTER 6

1. "The purpose of the wrestle was never punishment or the pain, fear, or confusion it brought. The point of the wrestle was to encounter the one who invited us to wrestle in the first place—the one who has been with us in it all along" (page 102). Have you found this to be true as you discovered God's purposes in your season of wrestling? In what ways have you experienced God more intimately in the midst of your pain?

2. What does it look like today for you to endure by faith and wrestle for the blessing? What is one small thing God might be asking you to do as a declaration that you believe His promises?

CHAPTER 7

1. Who do you believe you are, at the core? Who does God say you are? In what people, places, or activities (even serving God) have you sought to find your identity? Even if all these things were forever removed from your life, who does God say you are?

2. Are there particular places, people, or things in which you are misplacing your identity? What are the effects of this on your emotions and thoughts?

3. Scripture says confession and repentance lead to times of refreshing, deliverance, and proof of God's love—all things

our souls desperately need. In what ways, if any, might God be inviting you to repent during your season of wrestling?

CHAPTER 8

1. What questions are you still asking God at this point in your wrestle?

2. What questions is God asking of you as you wrestle through your pain?

3. What true biblical identity do you sense God is calling you to walk in as a symbol of what you have overcome?

CHAPTER 9

1. Answer this question from the text: "What might choosing to trust God again require of you?" (page 148).

2. Try approaching your quiet time like the counselor Sarah encouraged: with hands open, simply receiving from God rather than performing for Him. What shifts in you when you approach intimacy with God in this way?

3. Identify something you're struggling with and try the concepts of reframing and rebuilding around that struggle. How might these practices help you trust God more?

CHAPTER 10

1. What are some changes God has made in you during the process of wrestling through your current struggle? How

has wrestling with the questions in this book shifted your perspective?

2. What are some blessings and changes you are still wrestling God for?

3. What is your limp—the mark of victory and weakness that reminds you of the wrestle you've been through? In what ways is it a blessing? How might it help you depend on God and tell others about His love?

CHAPTER 11

1. What are some reasons to keep trying even when you're tired? What might it look like in your life to keep moving forward the next time you're tired of trying?

2. What blessings have you begun to recognize as a result of your wrestle?

3. Who do you think might benefit from hearing your wrestling story? How might you go about telling it?

ACKNOWLEDGMENTS

I HAVE ALWAYS DREAMED OF WRITING A BOOK, and it has been both an amazing experience and much harder than I ever imagined. I could not have done it without the support of my husband and best friend, Daniel, who reminds me continually that when we were dating, I told him I wanted to do this—and now I have. Thank you, babe, for all the laundry you folded, the meals you cooked, the trips to the grocery store you made, and for the endless "I love you, too's." You will never stop being a gift to me. I love you.

To my boys, Ashton and Eisy, you are my heart and comedic relief. Thank you for being so willing to go with the flow in this season and for all the prayers we prayed about this book at your bedtimes. I love you.

To all my family, who walked through this wrestling season with me and weren't sure how to help me, thank you for loving me the best you knew how through such a hard time. You are my forever people, and I will continue to intercede for you in your own wrestling seasons. I love you.

Thank you to my small group girls, who consistently hyped me up, prayed big prayers with me, and listened over and over when I told you every week how I was "tired of trying." What a blessing you have been to me.

To my counselor, Meghann Goddard, thank you for the insights you have brought me and for the support you provided in this season that challenged me in ways I never expected. God has used you to guide me toward healing I didn't even know I needed. Thank you.

Thank you to Katie Hanes for always cheering for this book and for helping me in so many ways, both seen and unseen. Your skills are unmatched.

To my acquisitions editor, Jillian Schlossberg, and the entire team at Tyndale, thank you for taking a chance on me and this message. You have been so kind, supportive, and patient with me as I made my way through this process, and I know the Lord has paired us up for that reason. Thank you.

To my content editor, Christine Anderson, I knew immediately God placed you on this project with me to guide me through a place I had never been. This book would not be what it is without your help and eye for detail. Thank you for your patience with me and for pushing and helping me deliver this message. I so appreciate all your work. You are incredible at what you do, and I learned *so* much from you.

To the content strategy team at Proverbs 31 Ministries, I am so thankful for all the feedback you gave me throughout this process. I trust all of your insights and respect each of your opinions so highly. I will always be amazed and thankful for the opportunity to work closely with such talented women who love God so much and want to serve people well.

To Proverbs 31 Ministries as a whole and to Lysa TerKeurst, thank you for the opportunity to serve alongside you to eradicate biblical poverty and see what it means to be faithful stewards of the message of God from the inside out. The lessons I have learned from all of you who are experts in your fields have been invaluable to me, and I thank you for the wisdom I have gleaned from working with you over the years.

To my early readers, thank you so much for your willingness to read through this as I wrote it and to give me your feedback over those months. You are a visible representation of who I wanted to write this book for, and your words and insights have been woven deeply throughout these pages.

To my social media friends who have walked with me and read my words for years, thank you. Thank you for allowing me to be honest about my struggles and thank you for being honest about yours. What a gift it is to have friends whom I have never met and yet who know what it means to cheer for one another as we continue to get back up and believe the Lord again.

NOTES

CHAPTER 1: WHEN YOU'RE FRUSTRATED

1. *Easton's Bible Dictionary*, s.v. "Jacob," accessed via Bible Study Tools, https://www.biblestudytools.com/dictionary/jacob/.
2. Dictionary.com, s.v. "supplanter," https://www.dictionary.com/browse/supplanter.
3. *Merriam-Webster*, s.v. "steadfast," https://www.merriam-webster.com/dictionary /steadfast.
4. *Merriam-Webster*, s.v. "frustration," https://www.merriam-webster.com/dictionary /frustration.

CHAPTER 2: WHEN GOD HURTS YOUR FEELINGS

1. Clive Staples Lewis, *The Letters of C. S. Lewis* (New York: Harcourt Brace Jovanovich, 1966), 285.
2. Matt Krumrie, "What Makes a Great Wrestler," Team USA Wrestling, February 12, 2019, https://www.teamusa.org/USA-Wrestling/Features/2019/February/12/What -Makes-a-Great-Wrestler.

CHAPTER 3: WHEN GOD REVEALS UNHEALTHY ROOTS

1. Viktor E. Frankl, *Man's Search for Meaning* (Boston, MA: Beacon Press, 1959, 1962, 1984, 1992, 2006, 2014), 62.

CHAPTER 4: WHEN YOU CAN NO LONGER PRETEND

1. Warren W. Wiersbe, *Be Authentic: Exhibiting Real Faith in the Real World* (Colorado Springs, CO: David C. Cook, 1997), 58.

2. Herbert E. Ryle, *Cambridge Bible for Schools and Colleges* (Cambridge, England: Cambridge University Press, 1921), accessed on Bible Hub, https://biblehub.com/commentaries/genesis/32-24.htm.

3. "Relationships: Creating Intimacy," Better Health Channel, undated, https://www.betterhealth.vic.gov.au/health/healthyliving/relationships-creating-intimacy.

4. *Encyclopedia of the Bible*, s.v. "theophany," accessed via Bible Gateway, https://www.biblegateway.com/resources/encyclopedia-of-the-bible/Theophany.

5. Matthew Henry, *Matthew Henry's Concise Commentary*, accessed on Bible Hub, https://biblehub.com/commentaries/1_kings/19-9.htm.

CHAPTER 5: PRACTICING SURRENDER

1. "Grappling hold," Wikipedia, https://en.wikipedia.org/wiki/Grappling_hold.

2. Tony Evans, "Jacob: The Deceiver God Used," Tony Evans Sermons, April 5, 2016, YouTube video, https://www.youtube.com/watch?v=JBYBZqnwfTQ.

3. *Merriam-Webster*, s.v. "conceited," https://www.merriam-webster.com/dictionary/conceited.

4. *Merriam-Webster*, s.v. "surrender," https://www.merriam-webster.com/dictionary/surrender.

CHAPTER 6: ENDURING THE PAIN

1. Jay Robinson, AZ Quotes, https://www.azquotes.com/author/65364-Jay_Robinson#:~:text=Jay%20Robinson%20Quotes&text=Take%20a%20strong%20wrestler%2C%20get,is%20afraid%20of%20getting%20tired.

2. Author unknown, Quote Banner, https://quotebanner.com/quotes/author-unknown-quote-53214/there-is-no-glory-in-practice-but-without-practice-there-is-no-glory.

CHAPTER 8: CLINGING TO THE SAVIOR

1. William MacDonald, *Believer's Bible Commentary: A Complete Bible Commentary in One Volume*, 2nd ed., ed. Arthur L. Farstad (Nashville, TN: Thomas Nelson, 2016). Accessed via Bible Gateway, www.biblegateway.com.

2. "What is the meaning of the Hebrew Word Israel—Struggle or Prince?" Biblical Hermeneutics Stack Exchange, November 12, 2020, https://hermeneutics.stackexchange.com/questions/52966/what-is-the-meaning-of-the-hebrew-word-israel-struggle-or-prince-any-scholarl.

CHAPTER 9: BLESSED TO REBUILD TRUST

1. "Brené Brown on Empathy," RSA, December 10, 2013, YouTube video, https://www.youtube.com/watch?v=1Evwgu369Jw.

2. "Brené Brown on Empathy."

ABOUT THE AUTHOR

ASHLEY MORGAN JACKSON is an author and works full-time for Proverbs 31 Ministries, a nonprofit organization whose mission is to eradicate biblical poverty. She has also been ministering online through social media to her own community for over ten years. Her focus is communicating the grace and power of the truth of Christ and His Word to those whose faith feels fragile. Ashley spent several years battling mental health issues and questioning why a God she had served her whole life was allowing such pain. Through her own wrestling, she found the blessing in being broken and now desires to share with others the beauty of allowing God to do what He has come to do in our lives.

Ashley resides in Charlotte, North Carolina, with her husband, Daniel. They have two school-age sons. Her daily prayer is that the joy of the Lord would be their strength. Ashley enjoys hanging out with her family, traveling, graphic design, prayer journaling, and laughing till she can't breathe.

Follow Ashley on Instagram, TikTok, and her website, ashleymorganjackson.com.